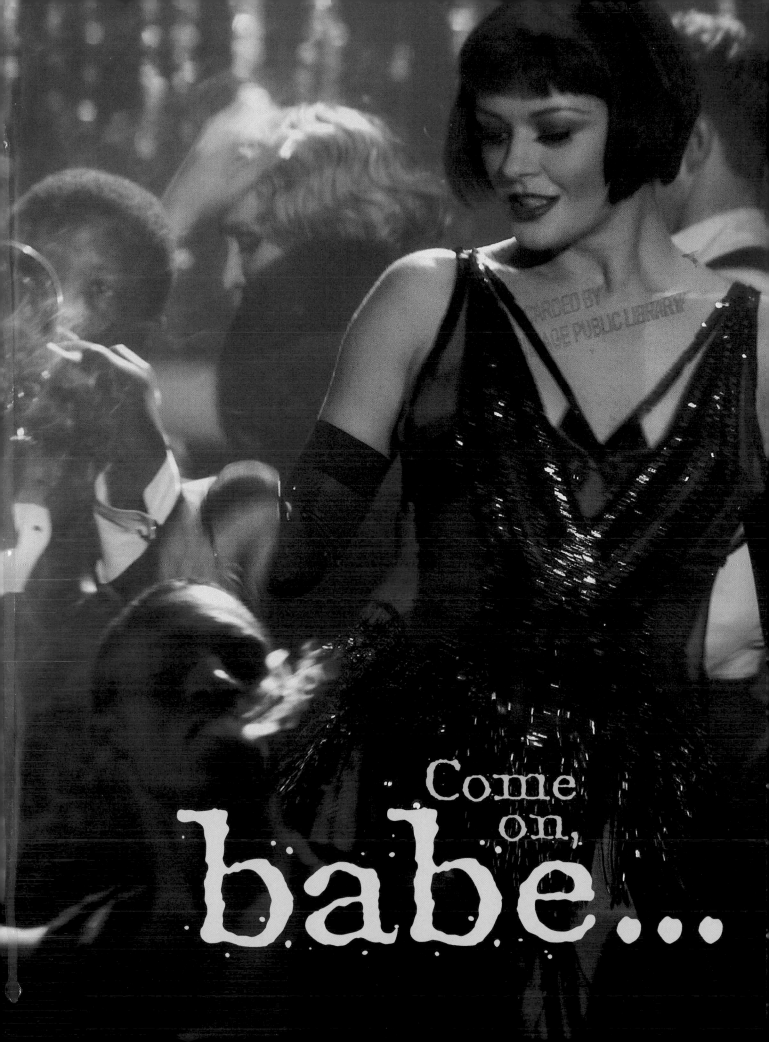

Come on,
babe...

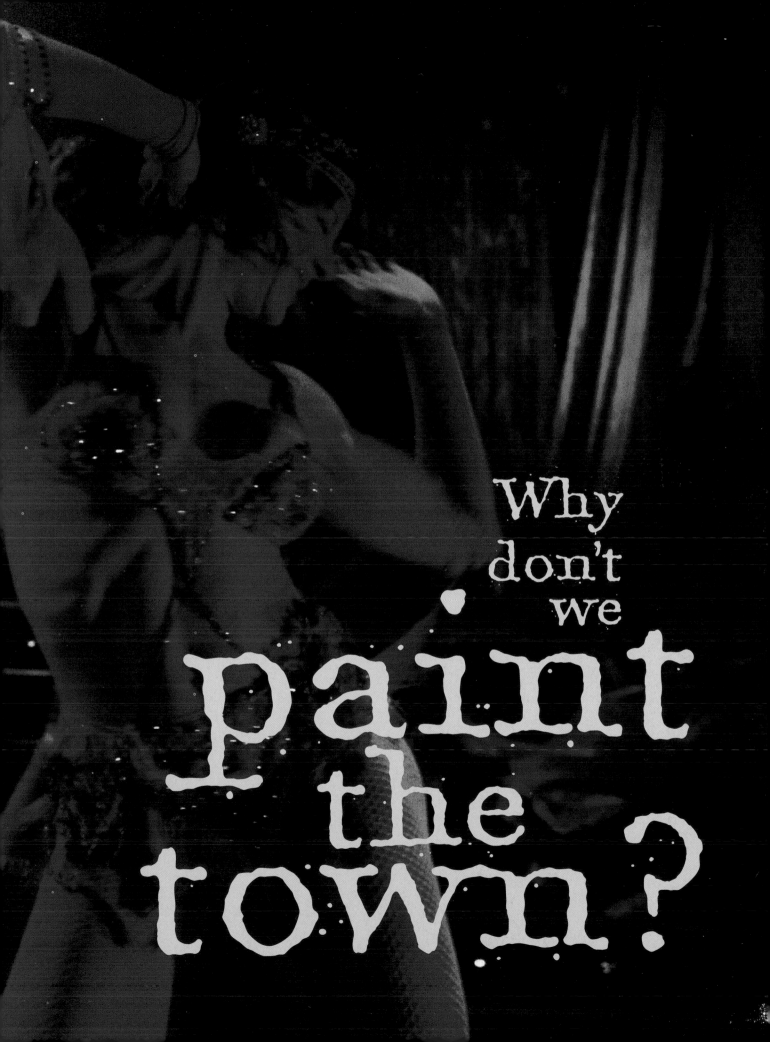

Why don't we **paint the town?**

And all that...

Jazz

CHICAGO

Introduction by **ROB MARSHALL**

Foreword by **BILL CONDON**

Preface by **MARTIN RICHARDS**

Screenplay by **BILL CONDON**

Lyrics by **FRED EBB**

Still Photographs by **DAVID JAMES**

Additional Photographs by
ALBERT WATSON, RAFY and PIERRE VINET

Text by **PETER KOBEL**

Designed by **TIMOTHY SHANER**

A NEWMARKET PICTORIAL MOVIEBOOK

NEWMARKET PRESS • NEW YORK

First Edition

10 9 8 7 6 5 4 3 2

Library of Congress Cataloging-in-Publication Data
available upon request.

ISBN 1-55704-578-X

www.newmarketpress.com

Design by Timothy Shaner.

Manufactured in the United States of America

QUANTITY PURCHASES
Companies, professional groups, clubs, and other
organizations may qualify for special terms when
ordering quantities of this title. For information, write
Special Sales Department, Newmarket Press,
18 East 48th Street, New York, NY 10017;
all (212) 832-3575; fax (212) 832-3629;
or e-mail mailbox@newmarketpress.com.

Other Newmarket Pictorial Moviebooks include:

contents

introduction

by Rob Marshall

I was fifteen when I first saw *Chicago* on the New York stage. I traveled from Pittsburgh, where I grew up, to see the show, and we knew one of the performers—a marvelous actress named Lenora Nemetz—in the Broadway production. She was hired by Bob Fosse to stand by for the leads, Gwen Verdon and Chita Rivera. I got to meet her backstage, and she showed us around. What a thrill that was for a kid! When Chita Rivera left the show, Lenora took over, and we went back and saw it again with her in it.

After seeing the performance, I listened to the album over and over and loved this musical more than words can convey. For me, *Chicago was* Broadway. And although it

wasn't my first Broadway show—I think *Gypsy*, with Angela Lansbury, was my initiation—it was certainly one of the very first I saw, and then *Chicago* was *it*. So it's a dream come true for me that I've come full circle, going from that little kid, the 15-year-old at the stage door, to directing this movie. Please forgive me for believing it's destiny.

How did all of this come about? Three years ago, I met with some Miramax executives to talk about filming a musical. I said, "Can I just tell you what I would do with the movie of *Chicago*?" I knew that Miramax cofounder Harvey Weinstein had the rights to it, and I had an idea of how it might work. So they said, "Let's go into Harvey's office." I met with Harvey and explained my concept—that it needed to take place in two worlds: a real one and an imaginary one. I was there for two hours, and I think Harvey knew then that this was the way to go.

And so they entrusted me with the film's development. Although I've been a stage director for many years, I'd never directed a theatrical film before. So we went looking for a writer. That proved more difficult than I'd imagined because it's hard to find people who've done this kind of thing before—librettos for musicals—because they're rarely done on film anymore. But the second I met Bill Condon, and we sat down at

LEFT: Rob Marshall with Renée Zellweger and Christine Baranski, in background, rehearsing for "We Both Reached for the Gun." ABOVE: A rehearsal workout.

11

the Four Seasons in L.A., I just knew I'd met a kindred spirit who loves musical theater and who knows it well. Bill had never scripted a musical before. But he'd had tremendous success with *Gods and Monsters*, which he wrote and directed and which, of course, won him an Oscar. It turned out that he loved *Chicago*, knew *Chicago*, and completely understood what I was trying to do with *Chicago*.

In some ways, *Chicago* is a very dark piece. It's fun and it's a great ride, but it has something important to say about our complicity in choosing our celebrities, the people we choose to celebrate. It's a satire, based on a play written by Maurine Dallas Watkins in the '20s that was also called *Chicago*. She worked as a cub reporter in Chicago covering all these so-called jazz slayings committed by women who became huge celebrities and sometimes got off scot-free. Her play opened on Broadway in 1926 and was a huge hit. People were laughing at it because it was actually happening then, and it's still happening now. It's a timeless piece. I mean, honest to God, if somebody said, "We want Linda Tripp and Monica Lewinsky to star in a big Broadway show," I bet they'd do it.

The songwriting team John Kander and Fred Ebb, who created the musical *Chicago* with Bob Fosse, transformed Watkins' original material. They don't just use their showbiz roots to entertain—they say something very significant, and very moving. I don't think there's anybody quite as good (they also collaborated on *Cabaret* and *Kiss of the Spider Woman*), and I'm fortunate to have worked with them as much as I have.

While working on *Chicago*, I've felt a great deal of responsibility in terms of the musical on film because some people have claimed that it's a dead genre. Musical theater is American-born, and it's our form. When musicals are done beautifully, like *Singing in the Rain* or *Cabaret* or *Bandwagon* or *Funny Girl*, it seems completely organic and convincing that people can sing and dance while telling their stories. When musicals are done right, they lift you in a way that no other form can. And that's why I love them so.

ABOVE: Rob Marshall replays a take as dancers look on.

"It's fun and it's a great ride, but it has

something important to say about our

complicity in choosing our celebrities,

the people we choose to celebrate."

—ROB MARSHALL

foreword

by Bill Condon

Before working on *Chicago*, I'd never written a musical, but I've always loved them. I grew up in New York and started seeing them in high school. And that's why, when I heard that *Chicago* was finally going to be produced as a film, I really went after it.

Even though I've never worked in theater, I've always been a complete and total fan. Because I don't know the mechanics of theater, I feel like I've remained the same kind of fan I was when I was a teenager—it's all sort of mysterious to me. With film, once you start working in movies, you see how the little pieces go together, and you can never quite have that same feeling about it again. But theater's remained very pure for me.

What I love about musicals is the way that things become larger than life and the extraordinary way in which people express themselves—that wonderful combination of music, dance, design, and drama. I think that just at the time when I first discovered musicals they were growing up and becoming more sophisticated. In the late 1960s, *Cabaret* was one of the first examples of a new kind of musical called a "concept musical." The songs didn't forward the plot so much as comment on what you'd just seen. So in the *Cabaret* movie there would be a love scene between Liza Minnelli and Michael York, and then she'd go and sing a torch song on stage called "Maybe This Time," which expresses her deepest emotions, in counterpoint to what's happening between these two characters. The musicals I saw in high school, such as *Company* and *Follies*, were really very exciting, as exciting as anything else that was going on in theater at that time. So just as people call the early 1970s the golden age of movies, it was a golden age for musicals as well.

When I first met with director Rob Marshall, we discovered that we were both thinking about taking the same approach to adapting *Chicago* to film. I knew then just how much I wanted to work on this script and, luckily for me, Rob chose me to work with him.

In the original production of *Chicago*, the concept was basically "Life is vaudeville." Or, as Billy Flynn says, "It's all a circus, kid. A three-ring circus. These trials—the

LEFT: Richard Gere, center, with dancers. ABOVE: Screenwriter Bill Condon with Chita Rivera, left, and Renée Zellweger.

15

whole world—all show business." The characters did
vaudeville turns, which commented on the action, each
inspired by a famous act. What made this so brilliant was
that the form the musical took also expressed its basic
point—that our institutions, especially our legal system, are
just as tawdry as the cheapest act on the bill. It was a dark
vision and a great achievement.

But *Chicago* made for a difficult adaptation to movies,
for one simple reason. Remember, in *Cabaret*, Liza Minnelli
and Joel Grey played performers, which made it natural to
show them doing numbers—after all, it was part of what
they did every day. But in *Chicago*, the two leads, Roxie
(Renée Zellweger) and Velma (Catherine Zeta-Jones), are
sitting in jail for most of the story. And the other characters
have completely different professions. Billy Flynn (Richard
Gere) is a lawyer. Amos Hart (John C. Reilly) is a car
mechanic. Mama Morton (Queen Latifah) is a prison matron.
So that was the challenge. How is it possible to retain the
vaudeville metaphor that informed every single moment of
the play, when these characters had no reason to be on a
stage? In other words—how do you get them to sing?

Our answer was to make the musical world of the film
live in Roxie's imagination. Roxie is
someone who's obsessed with being on
the stage—being noticed. She has an
overly active fantasy life, and when
things get too unpleasant, she projects
herself out of reality and re-imagines
the experience as a vaudeville number.

On stage, all of *Chicago* is a vaudeville. Not only the numbers, but also
the book scenes, which are highly stylized. But the central conceit of the

movie—that the musical numbers represent Roxie's escape from reality—meant that there had to be a real world for her to escape from.

The basic approach also demanded that Roxie become more central than she is in the play. After all, we're seeing everything through her eyes. And movies demand that a central character be someone you engage with on some level. The challenge was to make Roxie more human and real without softening her. What makes her so compelling is that she's a shrewd, ambitious animal, and I was hell-bent on not losing any of that nastiness. For anyone who loves *Chicago*, that would have been a betrayal.

I'm amazed by how enduring this little story has turned out to be. It has resonated in different ways over the years. Maurine Dallas Watkins' original 1926 play ushered in a generation of cynical, wise-cracking newspaper comedies. It was made into a successful movie (*Roxie Hart*) in the '40s. In 1975, Bob Fosse cast a darker light on the material. The corruption of the legal system became a metaphor for the hollowness of all American institutions. Like so much popular art of the time, it was

informed by the twin traumas of Vietnam and Watergate. Then *Chicago* was revived in 1996, on the heels of the O. J. Simpson case, and the show business metaphor really came into focus. After all, we'd just seen how the legal system could be manipulated by an expert showman.

This new version, I hope, is one for our times.

Preface

by Martin Richards

Chicago was my very first Broadway musical. Producer Bobby Fryer asked me to be his partner on it. "I'm doing a show," he said, "with Bob Fosse, Gwen Verdon, and Chita Rivera." And I thought, "Oh, my God." So I danced it, and sang it, and played it for everyone I knew. And my family started raising money, my friends were raising money, and we raised all the money, and we had a big hit.

We were nominated for eleven Tony Awards in 1976 against a show that was nominated for twelve Tonys, a little show called *A Chorus Line*. As it turned out, we didn't win a single award, and *A Chorus Line* went home with nine. Well, that's water under the bridge.

When we did *Chicago* in the mid-1970s, it was considered a very offbeat musical, and some people thought, You don't do musicals about murderesses. It took O. J.

Simpson for everyone to really understand *Chicago*. That's because a lot of people had trouble figuring out what the heck was happening with yellow journalism, and murder trials, and people singing and dancing. But now there are all these bestselling books and made-for-TV movies based on real-life murders and murder trials being televised. So *Chicago* found its time.

Chicago is all about murder and greed and debauchery—everything we hold near and dear to our hearts. It's everything that's happening today in the papers. It's today's headlines. It's the six o'clock news.

Although it's taken what seems like ages for this movie to reach the screen, in the end it all just fell into place in the right way. It's like a late birth with a baby that arrives right on time. It's been a joy.

ABOVE: Renée Zellweger and Martin Richards, center. RIGHT: From left, Catherine Zeta-Jones, Martin Richards, Neil Meron, Renée Zellweger, Richard Gere, and Craig Zadan. Photo by Albert Watson.

Right from the Headlines

While it took more than a quarter-century for the musical *Chicago* to go from stage to screen, its story actually goes back much further, to the raucous, roaring '20s when a young woman was hired by the *Chicago Tribune* to cover crime from a "feminine" perspective.

As a cub reporter for the *Tribune*, Maurine Dallas Watkins was assigned to the police beat. And she was on the job on March 12, 1924, when two Chicago cops found a man shot to death in a car owned by Mrs. Belva Gaertner, a twice-divorced cabaret singer. At first Gaertner denied any knowledge of the killing, but after acknowledging that the gun found in the car was hers, she cannily answered all questions with "I don't know. I was drunk." The dead man, Walter Law, left behind a widow. He had "made [Gaertner's] acquaintance," Watkins wrote, "through an automobile sale and retained it through midnight gin escapades."

Watkins saw an opportunity to get the story out of the police blotter and onto the front page. She spiced it up with a wry wit and sophisticated tone, and Gaertner did her part by providing great quotes, like "Gin and guns—either one is bad enough, but together they get you in a dickens of a mess." If not the first writer to hit on the murder-as-entertainment formula, Watkins was certainly savvy about exploiting it. She was soon assigned to cover the trial for the *Tribune*.

Watkins, who had a mix of pluck and luck, happened on another strangely similar case less than a month later. On April 3, a married woman shot and killed her lover. Watkins' page one story, under the headline "Woman Plays Jazz Air as Victim Dies," began, "For more than two hours yesterday afternoon Mrs. Beulah Annan, a comely young wife, played a foxtrot record named 'Hula Lou' in her little apartment at 817 East 46th Street. Then she telephoned her husband and reported that she had killed a man who 'tried to make love' to her." Annan, whom Watkins called the "prettiest murderess,"

LEFT: Pedestrians on State Street, Chicago, Illinois, 1928. ABOVE: Men reading newspapers outside the Chicago Daily News *building, 1928.*

23

Maurine Dallas Watkins

Maurine Dallas Watkins' first—and last—full-time newspaper job lasted just six months in 1924. But her $50 a week stint as a crime reporter at the *Chicago Tribune* provided fodder for a big Broadway play that tells a story that still resonates today.

Born in 1896 in Louisville, Watkins was the only child of a minister and a schoolteacher. She graduated from Butler University in Indianapolis before attending graduate school at Radcliffe College, where she first took George Pierce Baker's playwriting class.

An attractive woman who wore her hair braided rather than fashionably bobbed, Watkins didn't finish her master's, but instead moved to Chicago. At the *Tribune*, she quickly got her stories, stylishly written with a sardonic wit, onto the front page. In a symbiotic relationship, she turned two "murderesses," Belva Gaertner and Beulah Annan, into celebrities, and they provided her with great copy.

She moved back to New York and re-enrolled in Baker's drama class, which he was then teaching at Yale. There she penned her only successful play, *Chicago*. It ran

on Broadway and toured other cities, including Chicago. Watkins wrote a number of plays, but never managed to repeat her early success (her 1927 play *Revelry*, adapted from a novel about the Teapot Dome scandal and the Harding administration, had a brief New York run).

Like many writers, Watkins then tried her hand at screenwriting in Hollywood, where she lived during the 1930s. She worked on a number of films, but had only one unequivocal hit, the 1936 screwball comedy *Libeled Lady*. Directed by Jack Conway and starring Myrna Loy, Spencer Tracy, and Jean Harlow, it follows the machinations of a newspaper editor out to get some dirt on an heiress.

In the early 1940s after the death of her father, Watkins moved to Florida, where she grew obscure and eccentric. She never married and wore a veil in public. Although there was still interest in the rights to *Chicago*, she refused to sell them. When she died in 1969, she left behind an estate valued at more than $2 million, but she was so forgotten that the *New York Times* didn't bother to print her obituary.

claimed that she and her lover had had an argument. While struggling over a gun, it went off and he was killed.

Annan proved to be a cunning defendant. The day after another inmate, an illiterate immigrant, was sentenced to life for murder, Annan announced that she was with child (Illinois law prohibited the death sentence for pregnant women). Her attorney managed to get her an all-male jury—four of them bachelors—and she entered a plea of self-defense. As Watkins put it, "Beulah Annan, whose pursuit of wine, men, and jazz music was interrupted by her glibness with the trigger finger, was given freedom last night by her 'beauty proof' jury." Then it was Gaertner's turn. "Cook county's most stylish defendant," as Watkins described her, broke into hysterical laughter after being acquitted.

But the clever young newspaperwoman had ambitions beyond page one. Before the end of the year, she quit her job at the *Tribune* and moved to New York. There she started commuting to Yale, where she enrolled in George Pierce Baker's playwriting class to help her transmute her reporting into a stage satire. The result was *Chicago*, originally titled *Play Ball*, which drew closely on her trial coverage. The freed murderesses, glamorized by Watkins in her newspaper writing, became the characters Velma Kelly and Roxie Hart. The shyster lawyer Billy Flynn was based on Annan's attorney, W. W. O'Brien; the *Chicago Post* later noted that several of Billy Flynn's lines came directly from O'Brien's defense of Annan.

So Watkins conjured her tale of the murderess Roxie Hart, who is coached by her attorney to "go out for sympathy through the press." *Chicago*, directed by George Abbott, premiered in New York on December 30, 1926, and received good reviews. It was funny, and it had bite. The *New York Times'* Brooks Atkinson wrote, "*Chicago...* is a satirical comedy on the administration of justice through the fetid channels of newspaper publicity—of photographers, 'sob sisters,' feature stunts, standardized prevarication and generalized vulgarity." He summed up the play as "a raucous lampoon."

The following year, Cecil B. DeMille supervised a silent film version of the play that was directed by Frank Urson. In 1942, Ginger Rogers starred in another film version, *Roxie Hart*, directed by William A. Wellman. Rogers' incarnation of Roxie is a bit more sympathetic: She doesn't actually commit a murder; instead she agrees to be

LEFT: Playright Maurine Dallas Watkins. ABOVE: Belva Gaertner in jail, 1924.

Real-Life Murderess Row

Belle Brown Overbeck Gaertner (a.k.a. Belva Gaertner), a cabaret singer, had been married three times to two men. She had married and divorced a man named Overbeck, then had married William Gaertner, a rich manufacturer of scientific instruments. The marriage was a society affair, but was annulled five months later when it was discovered that she had been divorced less than a year. She and Gaertner remarried, and the union lasted three years. Both husband and wife had hired multiple detectives to spy on one another.

Gaertner, "about 38," had taken up with Walter Law, 29, a married man, after buying a car from him. She said she was too drunk to remember what had happened the night Law was found shot to death in her car with her gun. The prosecution portrayed Law as "a boy who couldn't refuse" the twin temptations of women and gin, and said that he had tried to break off their relationship when Gaertner shot him after "three months of wild gin parties," according to Maurine Watkins' news reports. But, Gaertner said, "It's silly to say I murdered Walter. I liked him and he loved me—but no woman can love a man enough to kill him. They aren't worth it, because there are always plenty more."

After she was acquitted, she laughed, threw her arms around her attorneys, and thanked the jury. She said that she planned to remarry her former husband and then travel to Europe. One of the other women on "murderesses' row" at the Cook County Jail, numbering just four after Gaertner's and Beulah Annan's acquittals, said, "The place ain't the same without her," for she was the best dancer and card player. She also hired other women to wash and iron her clothes.

Beulah May Annan, 23, shot and killed her lover, Harry Kalstedt, 29, then called her husband a few hours later claiming that he'd "tried to make love" to her. She initially told police the same story, then

RIGHT: Belle Brown Overbeck Gaertner (a.k.a. Belva Gaertner), 1924, the inspiration for Velma Kelly. CENTER RIGHT: Beulah May Annan, 1924, the real "Roxie Hart."

RIGHT: *Cook County Criminal Court building and jail.*
BELOW RIGHT: *The electric chair of Cook County jail,
Chicago, 1927.*

admitted that she'd been "fooling around" with Kalstedt for two months and, after drinking a lot of gin in the morning, had shot him when he said he was leaving her. Later, she revised her story to say that during a quarrel they had both reached for the gun and that she'd killed him in self-defense.

After she was acquitted, the Assistant State's Attorney sighed, "Another pretty woman gone free." Two months after the trial, Annan divorced her husband to marry a publicist, whom she divorced after five months. She died in a sanatorium four years later.

27

the fall guy for a murder committed by her husband as a publicity stunt to boost her dance hall career. The comedy was well cast. Backing up the stunning Rogers were Adolphe Menjou as lawyer Billy Flynn and George Montgomery as a smitten reporter.

Gwen Verdon, the Broadway dancer who was married to director-choreographer Bob Fosse, had long wanted to do a show based on *Roxie Hart*. But Watkins, who had become a born-again Christian and eccentric recluse, refused to sell the rights to *Chicago*. Was Watkins remorseful about having helped to get the merry murderesses off scot-free and then making money off their crimes, as many have suggested? Or did she feel her work was misunderstood as a glorification of a decadent lifestyle when she intended a serious social satire? At one time, at least, she said she believed that it was "an honest attempt to say something I believed terrifically."

Whatever Watkins thought, it was not until her death in 1969 that the rights were secured for Fosse's musical production of *Chicago*, and the director-choreographer didn't

begin working on the project until 1973. He asked the composer-lyricist team John Kander and Fred Ebb to write the songs. Fosse and Ebb cowrote the book, coming up with the ingenious idea of setting Watkins' play on a vaudeville stage. And, of course, Verdon was to star as Roxie Hart. Chita Rivera would play the other pretty jailbird, Velma Kelly, and Jerry Orbach would be the mercenary, silver-tongued lawyer Billy Flynn.

But just as rehearsals were getting under way, the hard-working, hard-living director had a heart attack. The entire production came to a stop. Serious efforts were made to find temporary work for the actors, and coproducer Martin Richards' casting agency was able to help some of them out with jobs. Rivera put together a nightclub act to tide her over.

Three months later when Fosse walked into the rehearsal studio, the cast and production team burst into wild applause, but Fosse's brush with death seemed to have changed him. "The show got much darker," Kander has said. "Even though it had been acerbic, there was originally a certain joyous quality. After the heart bypass, he was going for something else than what we had started to do."

ABOVE: *Ginger Rogers as Roxie Hart, 1942.* RIGHT: *The hard-working, hard-living Bob Fosse.*

Bob Fosse

Director-choreographer Bob Fosse was born in 1927 in Chicago, the son of a vaudeville entertainer. He started taking classes in tap, jazz, and ballet at the age of nine, and while still a child began tap dancing and telling jokes in seedy nightclubs. By the age of thirteen, he was sharing billings with burlesque acts.

After World War II, Fosse formed a dance act, performing in hotels around the country and dancing on Sid Caesar's TV variety program, *Your Show of Shows*. In the early 1950s, he was a dancer and actor in several films, including *Kiss Me Kate*.

In 1954, Fosse choreographed the Broadway hit *The Pajama Game*, winning a Tony Award and establishing his signature look: bowler hats, white gloves, and pelvic thrusts. The following year he choreographed another hit, *Damn Yankees*. Fosse choreographed film versions of both musicals.

He directed his first Broadway musical, *Redhead*, in 1959, and subsequently directed a string of hits—*How to Succeed in Business Without Really Trying*, *Sweet Charity*, *Cabaret*, and, of course, *Chicago*.

In 1973 he was the first to win the showbiz triple crown: He won three Emmys for directing, producing, and choreographing a Liza Minnelli concert, *Liza with a Z*, an Oscar for directing the film version of *Cabaret*, and two Tonys for directing and choreographing *Pippin*.

In the semi-autobiographical film *All That Jazz,* Fosse foretold his death: The movie's chain-smoking director-choreographer, Joe Gideon, dies of a heart attack. Fosse himself died of a massive heart attack in 1987 in Washington, D.C., at the age of 60, on opening night of a revival of *Sweet Charity*.

Broadway theaters observed a minute of silence in his honor.

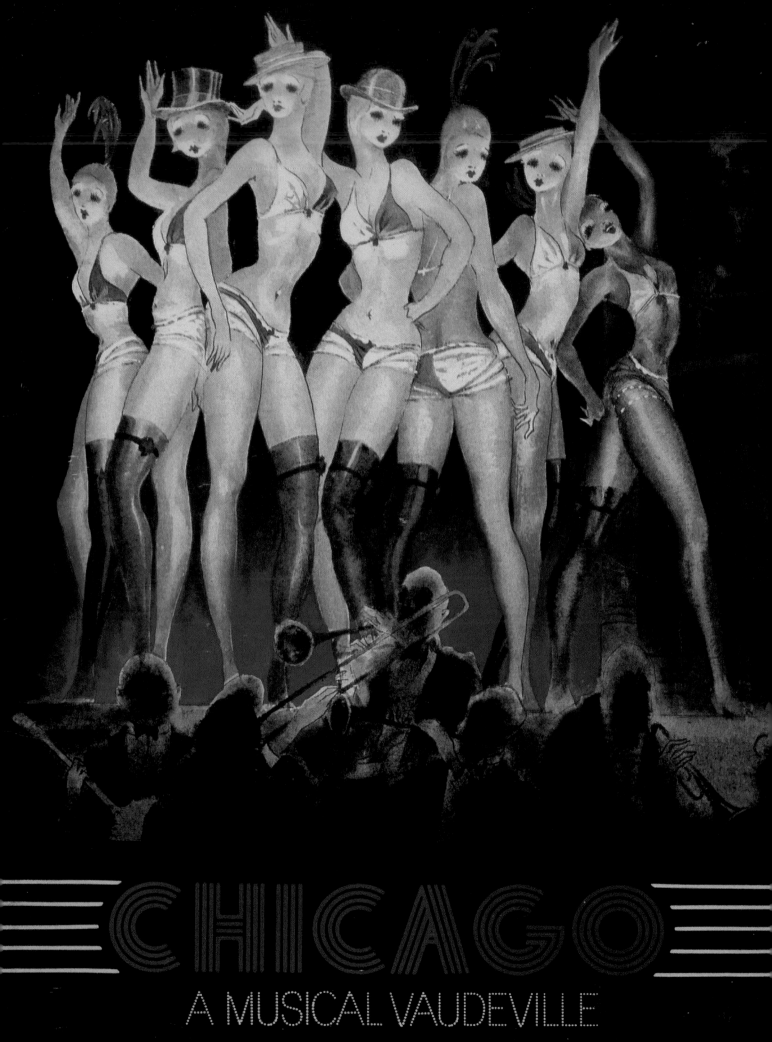

Chicago had its out-of-town run in Philadelphia in late 1974 before going to Broadway. The audience was very enthusiastic, but the reviews were bad. Fosse was undismayed. "When we originally opened in Philadelphia," says Richards, "a headline said, *Roxie Hart has no heart*. And then we all met and said, 'Bobby, you gotta do something about this.' He said, 'We'll discuss it tomorrow.' And we came in and talked about it, and he said, 'They're damn right. Roxie Hart has no heart, and we're taking out any heart that's in it. That's not what it's about.'"

So Fosse brought his brilliant, dark satirical show to New York—arguably the high point of his entire scintillating career. On the day the critics were to come, the cast ran through the play one last time. Fosse stood up and said simply, "You're all wonderful."

LEFT: Original program cover from Bob Fosse's 1975 production. TOP: Chita Rivera, left, and Gwen Verdon in 1975. Photo by Martha Swope. BOTTOM: "We Both Reached for the Gun," from 1975. Jerry Orbach, seated, as Billy Flynn. Photo by Martha Swope.

Kander and Ebb

Fred Ebb (left) and John Kander

John Kander and Fred Ebb comprise the longest-running songwriting partnership in Broadway musical history. Although composer Kander and lyricist/book writer Ebb had worked separately on various shows and revues, they only really became successful after joining together. Their first Broadway collaboration, 1965's *Flora, the Red Menace*, starred Liza Minnelli in her first leading role.

While *Flora* was not a hit, their collaboration the following year, *Cabaret*, certainly was. Set in pre-war Berlin during the Nazis' rise to power, the funny and unsettling show had a Broadway run of 1,166 performances, winning a Tony Award for Best Musical. The film version, directed by Bob Fosse, won eight Academy Awards. The 1998 Broadway revival, co-directed by Sam Mendes and Rob Marshall, won four Tonys, including Best Revival.

Celebrated for their extraordinary ability to produce musicals that are both deeply entertaining and have something to say, Kander and Ebb also composed the songs for *Chicago* (Ebb also cowrote the book with Fosse) and *Kiss of the Spider Woman*.

They have written for such films as Barbra Streisand's *Funny Girl* sequel, *Funny Lady*, and their title song for Martin Scorsese's *New York, New York* became an enormous hit and was quickly adopted as New York City's unofficial theme song.

Kander, 75, and Ebb, 67, composed a new song for the film of *Chicago* called "I Move On." Sung by Renée Zellweger and Catherine Zeta-Jones, it plays over the movie's credits.

Over all the years, Ebb once told *Newsday*, "We've never had an argument. Certainly we disagree. We're very dissimilar in our tastes; everything about us personally is very different. But when we work and if John loved a song that I thought was uhhh... I would still go along with him. And the same goes true I know for him."

Harold Prince, who directed *Cabaret* on Broadway, described the duo's contribution simply but well: "They write Broadway—in the best sense."

Liza Minnelli

Sandy Duncan

Marilu Henner

The show opened at New York's 46th Street Theater on June 3, 1975. *Chicago* followed Watkins' basic story fairly closely, while imposing its larger show business concept (highlighted by the new production's subtitle, "A Musical Vaudeville"). In this "story of murder, greed, corruption, violence, exploitation, adultery, and treachery," Roxie Hart (Verdon) is jailed after shooting her boyfriend. At the prison, run by Mrs. Morton, she meets Velma Kelly (Rivera)—who had only a small role in Watkins' play— and learns about the press-manipulating lawyer Billy Flynn (Orbach). Flynn, who claims he could have "gotten Jesus off if he had $5,000," helps Roxie spin her story to sob sister journalist Mary Sunshine. After her acquittal, Roxie and Velma hit the vaudeville circuit; in fact, the entire musical plays like a series of acts in a vaudeville theater.

Reviews were mostly positive, but some critics were put off by the musical's cynicism. Still, its biting humor, compelling musical numbers, and extraordinarily energetic dance sequences electrified audiences. It played 898 performances on Broadway, and then went on to a number of overseas productions.

Chicago was nominated for eleven Tony Awards in 1976, but was shut out by *A Chorus Line*, which swept the awards that year.

After a successful concert version was staged by the Encores! Series at New York's City Center in May 1996, the *Chicago* revival returned to Broadway in November. The revival opened with Ann Reinking playing Roxie, Bebe Neuwirth as Velma, James Naughton as Billy, and Joel Grey as Amos, Roxie's long-suffering husband. It was directed by Walter Bobbie and choreographed by Reinking.

The longest-running revival in Broadway history, *Chicago* won six Tony Awards in 1997, including Best Revival, Best Actor (Naughton), and Best Actress (Neuwirth).

Chicago: Starring...
4 Roxies, 1 Velma, 3 Billys

Ann Reinking

Bebe Neuwirth

James Naughton

Billy Zane

Taye Diggs

Vaudeville

Born in beer gardens, honky-tonks, and smoke-filled halls, vaudeville was a distinctively American form of popular entertainment from the mid-1890s to the early 1930s, when talkies and the Depression caused its rapid decline. A typical bill consisted of some 10 to 15 acts, which might include opera singers, burlesque dancers, blackface minstrels, trained animals, comedians, tightrope walkers, or whip snappers. Many future stars, such as W. C. Fields and Will Rogers, got their start there.

By the turn of the century, a system of vaudeville chains had been established, and many halls, like the Palace Theatre in New York, were quite impressive. An act would be hired to travel the chain's circuit, performing at halls in different towns (each act paid for its own travel expenses).

The premier circuits (those with the best venues and that paid the best) were known as the "big time." Only a few acts made the big time, of course, and those that didn't often had to play "the dumps," seedy halls across the country. Sometimes, a vaudevillian might be compelled to travel "the Death Trail," a string of shabby theaters running from Chicago to the Northwest and then down the West Coast to Los Angeles. Like show business today, vaudeville was a tough business.

In choosing vaudeville as the main structural device for their musical, Bob Fosse and Fred Ebb used it as a flexible metaphor for the killer competition of show business and the razzle-dazzle show business of journalism and the courts. Appropriately, vaudeville also had the element of the con, as when acts would "milk the audience," pretending to be on the verge of doing an encore to spur applause.

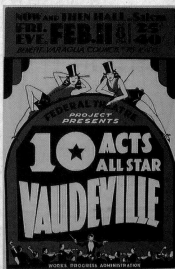

"The vaudeville form of *Chicago* aggressively reinforces the plot," playwright A. R. Gurney wrote in the *New York Times*. "Every song and dance is staged as a kind of number performed on the Orpheum circuit. The audience, in turn, becomes an essential element in the theatrical transaction: we are entertained, seduced, teased and at the same time mocked into seeing ourselves as the 'public' that Roxie Hart is playing to, to save her life."

Entertainment is a kind of con, the *Chicago* musical seems to be saying, and we are happy to be conned. And *Chicago*, like the best vaudeville, entertains and cons us big time.

ABOVE and RIGHT: Federal Theatre Project posters from the 1930s.
FACING PAGE: Recreating the vaudeville look for the film.

Filming the Musical

Bob Fosse once told Martin Richards, coproducer of the 1975 *Chicago*, that he wanted to make a film out of his musical. "I think I can do it," he said. "But I don't want it to be an ordinary picture."

Fosse directed many movies during his lifetime—*Sweet Charity, Cabaret, Lenny, All That Jazz,* and *Star 80*—but he never got around to *Chicago*. When he died in 1987, Richards told himself the film would never happen.

But at least one person who saw the original Fosse musical thought otherwise. Harvey Weinstein, long before he founded Miramax, saw the show and told his date that night that he'd make a film of it someday. Happily, Richards was wrong, and Weinstein was right, even if it took more than a quarter of a century to bring the project to fruition.

In 1994, Richards signed with Weinstein to film the musical. But *Chicago* was to prove a tough nut to crack; it would still take seven years before the stars aligned to make it happen.

Making a film version of *Chicago* posed an extraordinarily difficult problem—a sort of Gordian knot that defeated any number of directors and writers. But when Rob Marshall met with Miramax executives about filming a musical, he began by talking about how he would handle a film version of *Chicago*. Weinstein was impressed, and Marshall got the job.

"The biggest problem," Marshall says now, "was how to take the songs from the stage to film—because they're created specifically for the theater. The original title was *Chicago, a Musical Vaudeville*. That's because everything was told in the vaudeville, including the scenes, which had a sort of vaudeville sensibility to them. So how do you take something innately theatrical and make it work in film?

"I knew that these songs had to take place on some kind of a stage. Because that's how they were created—to be presentational vaudeville

LEFT: Catherine Zeta-Jones prepares for "All That Jazz."
RIGHT: Director Rob Marshall gives Renée Zellweger some on-set directions.

numbers. To try and turn them into book numbers—a book number is when the song comes from the story and character and people sing it to each other—wouldn't work. This is much more Brechtian; these songs comment on what's happening and further the plot in a sort of stylized way."

Marshall's idea was simple, and simply brilliant. "The idea was to simultaneously have a story that takes place on a stage and a story in the reality of Chicago in 1929. In one narrative, you jump back and forth between two realities."

Marshall needed someone to help him flesh out his basic premise. Miramax suggested several writers, but when he met Bill Condon—writer-director of *Gods and Monsters*, for which he'd won an Oscar for best adapted screenplay—they felt an immediate rapport.

When the two met at the Four Seasons in Los Angeles, Condon, a theater lover, was thoroughly familiar with Marshall's body of work and was already a big admirer. "I knew *Kiss of the Spider Woman*—he did great work on that—and the brilliant revival of *Cabaret* that he did with Sam Mendes," says Condon.

"When I met with him it was interesting because I'd come up with a take, and he was so excited about his take that I never got to say too much. But what was exciting about it was that it was the same approach."

Their enthusiasm spontaneously combusting, they formed the idea that the songs would take place in the theater of Roxie Hart's mind. In her obsession with show business, she would interpret her life through songs on an imaginary stage. But although it now seems so right, so aesthetically perfect, the idea was really only one of several concepts that Marshall and Condon brainstormed. "We discussed many

ABOVE: *Richard Gere and Neil Meron.*

different ways into this concept," Marshall says. "But nothing seems sure and right until you test it and you get through the whole script."

Any number of ideas were considered but eventually discarded. One scenario was that the entire story would be told as a flashback as Velma and Roxie are about to go on stage for their big finale. Another possibility was that the songs they did on stage would be their show, conceived by them to tell the story of the lives. "But all these other ideas ultimately had holes in them," Marshall says.

In creating two separate worlds—an imaginary world of stage fantasy and a world of gritty reality—the film naturally took on more period detail. In fact, the stage productions were not really period pieces at all, but the film evokes real life and stage acts of the 1920s.

"Originally, in 1975, it was truly done as a series of vaudeville acts with costumes," says Condon. "And then when it was revived in '96 that was all stripped away, and it was just kind of a sexy, very dark, downtown kind of production. But as a movie, with our two worlds, and where one of them is real, that meant that when we went into this fantasy, the songs really had to feel like numbers that were taking place on a stage in the late '20s. I think in the design, the orchestration, and Rob's staging—there's been much more attention to the period."

Another change necessitated by adapting the play to the screen was that the score needed to be streamlined. Marshall found it personally very difficult: "It's so painful to touch any of the score, because I love the score so much. I directed the show on stage in Los Angeles. But, inevitably, with a movie, unless you want it to be over three hours long, you have to eliminate some of the score. I'm sure it was painful for Bob Fosse when he filmed *Cabaret*, because he had to eliminate seven or eight of the songs."

Marshall, who dropped six songs from the original musical, explained his criteria for keeping tunes in the film: "Any song that didn't completely relate to the story, that

ABOVE: Martin Richards, left, and Harvey Weinstein visit a rehearsal.

39

felt like it was an entertainment as opposed to an intrinsic part of the storytelling, we felt wasn't necessary."

In the end, one song was filmed that didn't make the theatrical cut— "Class," sung by Catherine Zeta-Jones—but it is on the cast album and it will be on the DVD. As compensation, fans of the songwriting duo John Kander and Fred Ebb, who composed the original *Chicago* score, were thrilled to hear a new song, "I Move On," played over the film credits.

The adaptation problem finally resolved, Condon refined and honed the script with Marshall for a year. The director was then able to turn his attention to casting the film.

For a big-budget movie musical, Marshall needed marquee movie actors with name recognition exceeding that of even the biggest Broadway stars. But with more movies becoming stage musicals than vice versa, there was no list of tried-and-true movie musical actors as there had been, say, in the '50s and '60s.

"It's very tricky to audition movie stars," says Marshall, "but this is such a specific thing. Nobody knew who could do what. Musicals aren't done, so I had no idea who could sing, no idea who could dance, no idea who could really pull off musical performance."

So Marshall turned first to an actress with sterling musical credentials, Catherine Zeta-Jones, who early in her career had sung and danced her way into the lead of a West End production of *42nd Street*. "Catherine has the stuff. She's a pro," Executive Producer Neil Meron says. "If she had been around in the '40s, the '50s, she would have been one of the leading ladies in film musicals."

For the role of Billy Flynn, Marshall turned to Richard Gere, another actor with musical experience. Gere began his acting career in the theater; he had played Danny in *Grease* and had performed in some rock musicals.

Gere, brimming with self-confidence, easily talked himself into the role. He had only one caveat. The script called for his lawyer character

RIGHT: *Richard Gere and Renée Zellweger in rehearsal.*
FOLLOWING PAGES: *Rob Marshall directs the chorines.*

to tap dance during his final arguments at trial, and Gere wasn't sure that he could do it. So Marshall arranged for Gere to take tap lessons from associate choreographer Cynthia Onrubia. He was an outstanding student: Gere's tap-dancing razzle-dazzles not just the jury but film audiences as well.

The role of Roxie Hart was crucial. While she was always the main character in the stage musical incarnations, she is even more central in the film because the songs are played in her imagination. The filmmakers also wanted to humanize her character.

"The challenge in the script," says Condon, "was to create a world that was more real, and to create in the character of Roxie somebody with some psychological complexity, somebody you might feel more for. Personally, I felt the tough part of that was not to betray who she is.

"It's very easy to soften characters in movies, where suddenly you're told these three things about somebody in the beginning—they have a pet, they're nice to their mother or something—and that's meant to make you think they're nice people, and make you like them. And we didn't want to do that with Roxie, because she's not. She's incredibly ambitious and she has a kind of complete self-absorption. But at the same time you kind of have to fill her out."

Marshall had "work sessions" with ten actresses (he carefully avoided calling them "auditions"). Among them was Renée Zellweger, who came by the rehearsal studio just to visit before agreeing to a work session. Zellweger watched the rehearsals for a while, and after everyone had left, said to Marshall, "Now show me that one step again."

"I started working with her on some choreography," Marshall says, "and I could tell, honest to God, within 30 seconds that she could do it, that she could dance it

ABOVE: Rob Marshall, Renée Zellweger, and Richard Gere. RIGHT: Dion Beebe, director of photography, center, with dancers (clockwise from lower left) Michelle Johnston, Melanie Gage, Vicky Lambert, and Tara Nicole.

because she's an athlete anyway. She was a cheerleader. So she has a great sense of her body and moves beautifully."

Marshall, however, still didn't know if Zellweger could sing. They had dinner that evening at the Four Seasons in New York, and just as everyone was leaving, Zellweger asked Marshall to teach her one of the musical's songs.

"It was sort of quiet in the restaurant, and so I started teaching her 'Nowadays.' We started singing it quietly, and then she started singing it a little louder. I mean it was quite embarrassing. Then she started singing some other songs she knew, like 'Somewhere Over the Rainbow,' and I was auditioning her right there in the restaurant. And it was like, Wow, she really can sing. We had found our Roxie because that was the actress I'd always wanted. I wanted an actress that had that great vulnerability, and that depth and comedy."

Chicago's stellar cast gradually came together as other actors came on board—Queen Latifah as Matron Mama Morton, John C. Reilly as Amos Hart, Christine Baranski as Mary Sunshine, Lucy Liu as Kitty, and in cameos, Chita Rivera as Nickie, and Taye Diggs as the bandleader.

Marshall spent three months choreographing and rehearsing dancers in a New York theater. He was also assembling an extraordinary production team, drawing from the worlds of theater and film: cinematographer Dion Beebe, whose credits include *Charlotte Gray* and *Holy Smoke*; production designer John Myhre, whose work on *Elizabeth* had earned an Oscar nomination; costume designer Colleen Atwood, three-time Oscar nominee for her work on *Sleepy Hollow, Beloved*, and *Little Women*; and the theatrical lighting team of Jules Fisher and Peggy Eisenhauer. Fisher, who has won seven Tonys, worked on Fosse's version of *Chicago*.

As Marshall's vision began to take shape, he presented a preview to Miramax and the film's producers. Myhre created a scale model of the film's Onyx Theater, where the dance numbers take place, and moved cardboard cutout characters around on the stage. Four dancers did their numbers as a pianist played the show's tunes. "I did it as a real show," Marshall says. Everyone was bowled over.

Sets were built in Toronto, and the film's stars gathered there for an extraordinary six weeks of rehearsal. First they learned their songs, which were recorded early on. Then, during filming, they lip-synced their numbers. The fourteen-hour days and six-day weeks of rehearsal were like musical boot camp.

"It was like school," says Zellweger. "There was first period, which was singing class. I would go to the piano room while Richard was at tap and Catherine was working on 'All That Jazz' on the main floor. Then we'd rotate. It was fantastic."

The intensity of the training resulted in a feeling of camaraderie more typical of a stage musical than a film. "What you get with a six-week rehearsal like that is a company," says Marshall, "a company with Queen Latifah, John C. Reilly, Christine Baranski, and all these wonderful dancers!"

For Marshall, who made his big-screen film debut with *Chicago*, it was like directing two projects at once. "It really was like directing a film and a musical simultaneously," he says. "In the end, hopefully, they're a seamless whole."

ABOVE: John Kander and Fred Ebb view a scale model of the "Cell Block Tango" set with Rob Marshall.
ABOVE LEFT: Detail of the scale model. LEFT: Renée Zellweger rehearses with Marshall.

Movie Illustrated & Lyrics

Cast

Catherine Zeta-Jones
Velma Kelly

Richard Gere
Billy Flynn

Renée Zellweger
Roxie Hart

PRICE TWO CENTS—48 PAGES

IN CHICAGO AND SUBURBS — ELSEWHERE THREE CENTS

JAZZ SLAYER

John C. Reilly
Amos Hart

Christine Baranski
Mary Sunshine

Queen Latifah
Matron Mama Morton

A five-six-
seven-eight...

CHICAGO

IN BLACKNESS
The slow, sexy wail of a jazz trumpet. FADE UP on:

ROXIE HART'S EYES, HEAVILY MADE-UP
Red stage lights are reflected in her eyes...the lights shining brighter as we move in closer... until one eye FILLS THE FRAME.

The lights get hotter still, almost searing. Bits of neon form a word:

CHICAGO

The screen goes black.

> **BANDLEADER** (V.O.)
> A five-six-seven-eight...

INT. THE ONYX THEATER - NIGHT (LATE 1920S)
On a small stage, the BANDLEADER — early '30s, dapper — plays the piano and leads an all-black jazz band in a scorching set. In a former life, this was a neighborhood vaudeville house; since the onset of Prohibition, the seats have been ripped out and tables moved in, turning the Onyx into a slightly seedy nightclub. As we move through the crowd, we see a few PATRONS spiking their drinks with bootleg hooch.

IN THE WINGS
A panicked STAGE MANAGER moves through the crowded backstage area.

> **STAGE MANAGER**
> Anybody seen the Kelly sisters?

A few CHORINES in skimpy costumes warm up in the wings. The stage manager checks out the other acts — the VENTRILOQUIST with his wooden doll; the skinny COMIC; the TRAMP act. He points to a loose-limbed ECCENTRIC DANCER.

> **STAGE MANAGER** (CONT'D)
> You're up in five.

EXT. THE ONYX - NIGHT
A bleak mid-winter night. A taxi pulls up to the curb and a WOMAN steps out. The longest legs you've ever seen, followed by a suitcase.

> **VELMA** (OFF-CAMERA)
> Keep the change, Charlie.

The woman stops in front of a bill. Tonight's headline act: THE KELLY SISTERS — VELMA KELLY & VERONICA KELLY — BACK BY POPULAR DEMAND! A gloved hand rips the bill in half, leaving only one name, VELMA KELLY.

INT. THE ONYX - STAGE - NIGHT
The band is jamming.

INT. THE ONYX - BACKSTAGE - NIGHT
MOVING behind the woman as the stage manager advances on her.

> **STAGE MANAGER**
> Velma, where ya been? And where's Veronica?

> **VELMA** (O.C.)
> She's not herself tonight.

Velma glides through the pandemonium.

> **STAGE MANAGER**
> But they paid to see a sister act.

> **VELMA** (O.C.)
> Don't sweat it. I can do it alone.

INT. THE ONYX - DRESSING ROOM - NIGHT
Velma's hands open the suitcase, which shows evidence of hasty packing. She lifts out stockings, pumps, a garter with a rhinestone buckle — as well as a pearl-handled revolver wrapped in a bloody handkerchief. (All we see are hands, legs, buckles, stockings, gun, and blood.)

INT. THE ONYX - STAGE - NIGHT
The vamp starts.

The following screenplay has been slightly abridged for this publication.

The Onyx Theater

Vaudeville wannabe Roxie Hart's song-and-dance fantasies transpire on the stage of the Onyx Theater, created by production designer John Myhre. First and foremost, the stage he would build in Toronto would have to accommodate the dancers' needs, so he spent a week in New York with director Rob Marshall and his dancers as they worked out the film's choreography.

Then as part of his research, Myhre also visited a number of New York theaters from the film's period. "One of the theaters we used as a basis for size and scale was Studio 54," Myhre says. "We were looking for something that was the opposite of what you'd normally find. We wanted a small auditorium, so that everything would be very intimate, and a big stage. We wanted a tight feel, with balconies almost overhanging the stage."

In addition to real New York theaters, Myhre turned to the paintings of Reginald Marsh for inspiration. A New York City artist, Marsh depicted Bowery bums and boxers, Coney Island crowds and subways, but he also painted New York theaters.

"He was a remarkable artist who painted the gritty scenes of New York in the '30s," Myhre says. "He did some wonderful theater scenes—not the glamorous houses, but the burlesque houses. There was this great compression to his paintings—every level was very compact and full of details. And it was what we were trying to

RIGHT INSETS: Concept illustrations for the Onyx Theater. RIGHT: The Onyx Theater set.

LEFT: Reginald Marsh's painting "Minsky's Chorus." ABOVE: Archival image of the Knickerbocker Theatre interior used in researching the look of the Onyx Theater.

get also, just the energy that comes out of his work. He really influenced every aspect of the production, from the set design to the lighting to the costumes."

In the interest of realism, Marshall and Myhre created a whole back story for the theater as well. "We decided that this Onyx Theater was once a working theater, maybe built around the turn of the century," Myhre says. "And then for some reason it was closed down or just left vacant for about 10 or 15 years until Prohibition came along. And then somebody had this idea of selling some bootleg hooch there and reopened it. But they didn't want to put any money into it."

And the Onyx onscreen conveys that vision, with its chipped gilded boxes and proscenium, the gold-edged crimson curtains, the worn black stage, and the flickering amber lights on round ebony tables. It's a perfect platform for Roxie's gritty, glamorous dreamscape.

BANDLEADER
Ladies and gentlemen, the Onyx Club
is proud to present Chicago's hottest
dancing duo, two jazz babes moving as one . . .

INT. THE ONYX - UNDER STAGE - NIGHT
Velma runs down the steps and jumps onto a wooden scissor lift. A couple of grizzled STAGEHANDS crank the wheel and the lift rises.

BANDLEADER
...the Kelly sisters.

On the bumpy lift, Velma notices a smudge of blood on her hand. She wipes it off and emerges into view, seeming to rise right out of the piano. Red cupid-bow lips and shiny Louise Brooks hair.

VELMA
COME ON, BABE
WHY DON'T WE PAINT THE TOWN?
AND ALL THAT JAZZ

There are two spots, one shining on Velma, the other where her sister Veronica should be.

VELMA (CONT'D)
I'M GONNA ROUGE MY KNEES
AND ROLL MY STOCKINGS DOWN
AND ALL THAT JAZZ

Velma cocks her head to the balcony. The second PROJECTIONIST rotates his heavy spotlight in Velma's direction.

Velma moves downstage, where MALE and FEMALE DANCERS are draped over tables and chairs, spent after a wild night of partying. It's as if the club itself has spilled onto the stage.

VELMA (CONT'D)
START THE CAR
I KNOW A WHOOPEE SPOT
WHERE THE GIN IS COLD
BUT THE PIANO'S HOT
IT'S JUST A NOISY HALL
WHERE THERE'S A NIGHTLY BRAWL
AND ALL...

The second spot has drifted again. Velma closes her hand, signaling the projectionist to take the light out.

VELMA (CONT'D)
THAT...

The dancers stir to life.

VELMA (CONT'D)
JAZZ!

BANDLEADER
SKIDOO.

VELMA
AND ALL THAT JAZZ.

ENSEMBLE
HOTCHA!

ENSEMBLE (CONT'D)
WHOOPEE!

VELMA
AND ALL THAT JAZZ!

A dance break:

ENSEMBLE
HAH! HAH! HAH!

We move through the crowd until we find ROXIE HART standing alone against a mural. She's strikingly pretty, especially in her slip of a black dress. There's also a whiff of desperation that no make-up or perfume can disguise.

VELMA
SLICK YOUR HAIR
AND WEAR YOUR BUCKLE SHOES
AND ALL THAT JAZZ!
I HEAR THAT FATHER DIP
IS GONNA BLOW THE BLUES
AND ALL THAT JAZZ

Roxie's eyes remain glued to the stage. She's so enraptured by the act, and by the sheer fact of being in this club — it's as though there's no other reality for her.

VELMA (CONT'D)
HOLD ON, HON
WE'RE GONNA BUNNY HUG
I BOUGHT SOME ASPIRIN
DOWN AT UNITED DRUG
IN CASE YOU SHAKE APART
AND WANT A BRAND NEW START
TO DO THAT —

ON STAGE (ROXIE'S FANTASY)
Roxie takes Velma's place on the stage. Same costume, same makeup, same hair.

I'm gonna rouge my knees And roll my stockings down

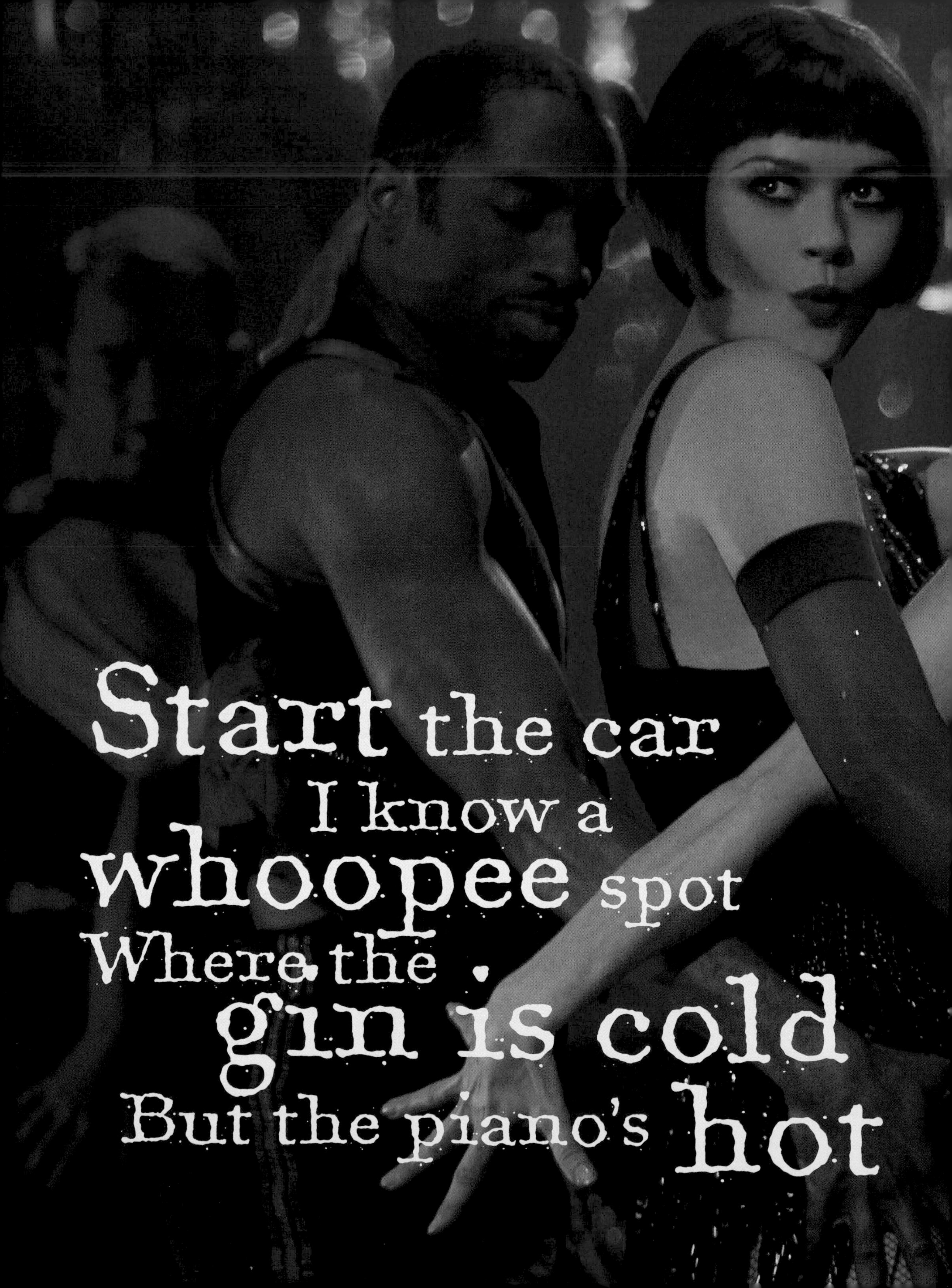

Start the car
I know a
whoopee spot
Where the
gin is cold
But the piano's hot

ROXIE
— JAZZ

Roxie sings and the crowd goes wild.

CASELY (V.O.)
Let's go, babe.

IN THE CLUB (BACK TO REALITY)
Roxie turns to see FRED CASELY heading for the door.

ROXIE
But I didn't even meet your friend.

Casely stuffs a wad of bills in his pocket.

CASELY
Don't worry, Roxie. It's all taken care of.

ROXIE
You told him about me?

CASELY
Yeah, kid, it's all arranged.

He pulls out a hip flask and grabs her ass. Velma slaps her own ass on stage.

VELMA
FIND A FLASK
WE'RE PLAYING FAST AND LOOSE
AND ALL THAT JAZZ!
RIGHT UP HERE
IS WHERE I STORE THE JUICE
AND ALL THAT JAZZ!
COME ON, BABE
WE'RE GONNA BRUSH THE SKY
I BETCHA LUCKY LINDY
NEVER FLEW SO HIGH

EXT. ALLEY - NIGHT
Roxie dodges traffic as she follows Casely to his car. The El train looms in the distance.

VELMA (V.O.)
'CAUSE IN THE STRATOSPHERE
HOW COULD HE LEND AN EAR

INT. THE ONYX - NIGHT

VELMA
TO ALL THAT JAZZ?

**INT. ROXIE'S APARTMENT BUILDING/ THE ONYX -
NIGHT (INTERCUT)**
MUSIC continues as Roxie leads Casely to her fifth-floor walk-up. (The rest of the number is INTERCUT between the apartment building and the Onyx.)

Catherine Zeta-Jones

Before Catherine Zeta-Jones became a movie actress she was a hoofer on the London stage, starring in *Annie* and *Bugsy Malone* and playing the lead in a West End revival of *42nd Street* when she was just seventeen. So performing in *Chicago* is like returning to her roots.

"I always used to tell my mom when I was a little girl that I wanted to be on the stage. And to me that was singing and dancing," Zeta-Jones says. "I was also obsessed with the golden years of Hollywood, the musicals. I would have loved that world—going to the set, having lunch with Fred, meeting up with Ginger for a cocktail. I used to say to my mother that I was born in the wrong era."

As the jazz killer/vaudeville performer Velma Kelly in *Chicago*, Zeta-Jones is indeed incarnated in a different era, the jazz-fueled, delirious '20s, but it's a time with its own strange and seedy glamour. In addition to the singing and dancing, she enjoyed evoking the period.

"That's the great thing about making movies," Zeta-Jones says. "You just take that world and re-create it. And that's what I've enjoyed, from the costumes to the whole kind of line delivery that they used to do in those days."

"The two characters, Roxie and Velma, have an interesting relationship," Zeta-Jones says. "Velma is this brash, brassy vaudeville singer who thinks she is the height of sophistication, and Roxie is the wide-eyed wannabe who's completely obsessed. She wants to be Velma. Throughout the story, the tides turn: Velma starts out on top, and then she's down in the gutter, and she builds herself back up. It's all about how desperate they are to top each other really."

In real life, the actresses worked together beautifully. The more experienced dancer-singer Zeta-Jones took the neophyte Zellweger under her wing, and the two formed a fast friendship on the set, even while reveling in their on-screen competition.

"I've loved working with Renée so much. It's like she was plucked out of a black-and-white photograph of the time, and put into Technicolor. She's done a phenomenal job on this. She's a great person to work off, and work with, and we had a lot of fun—catty, catty fun together."

"I always used to tell my mom when I was a little girl that I wanted to be on the stage. And to me that was singing and dancing."

VELMA (V.O.)
OH, YOU'RE GONNA SEE YOUR SHEBA
SHIMMY SHAKE

On stage, Velma is joined by two male dancers.

VELMA & ENSEMBLE
AND ALL THAT JAZZ

Casely reaches through a stair railing and runs his
hand up Roxie's leg.

VELMA (V.O.)
OH, SHE'S GONNA SHIMMY 'TIL HER
GARTERS BREAK

On stage, the male dancers reach for Velma's leg.

VELMA & ENSEMBLE
AND ALL THAT JAZZ

Casely stops on the top landing, out of breath. He
takes a nip from the flask, pours some down
Roxie's throat. His tongue scoops a trickle of gin
from her neck.

VELMA (V.O.)
SHOW HER WHERE TO PARK HER GIRDLE
OH, HER MOTHER'S BLOOD'D CURDLE

Roxie stifles a laugh, shushes Fred as they move
down the hall.

On stage, the ensemble slinks and slithers behind
Velma.

VELMA & ENSEMBLE (HUSHED)
IF SHE'D HEAR
HER BABY'S QUEER

VELMA
FOR ALL...

Casely pushes Roxie against a neighbor's door.

VELMA (CONT'D)
THAT...

Casely throws Roxie's arms up.

VELMA (CONT'D)
JAZZ!

The door cracks open. An unpretty older HOUSE-
WIFE, glowering.

ROXIE
Evenin', Mrs. Borusewicz.

NEIGHBOR
Mrs. Hart.

She gives Casely the once-over.

ROXIE
This is Fred. He's my brother.

A giggle and a hiccup as Roxie pushes Casely
toward her apartment.

VELMA
ALL...

Roxie opens her apartment door.

VELMA (CONT'D)
THAT...

She pushes Casely into the apartment.

VELMA (CONT'D)
JAZZ...

Roxie shuts the door.

The number really explodes now. Frenzied, sleazy,
and completely electric.

VELMA (CONT'D)
COME ON, BABE
WHY DON'T WE PAINT THE TOWN
AND ALL THAT JAZZ
I'M GONNA ROUGE MY KNEES
AND ROLL MY STOCKINGS DOWN
AND ALL THAT JAZZ

ENSEMBLE
OH, YOU'RE GONNA SEE
YOUR SHEBA SHIMMY SHAKE
AND ALL THAT JAZZ
OH, SHE'S GONNA SHIMMY
'TIL HER GARTERS BREAK
AND ALL THAT JAZZ

Roxie yelps in delight as Casely carries her across
the cheap railroad flat. He tosses her on the bed,
rips off her stockings and garters.

The band plays faster. Hotter.

More rough foreplay from Casely. Roxie comes up
for air, notices her husband Amos staring plaintive-
ly from a framed wedding photo. She slams the picture face down.

A montage of body parts — arched BACKS; curled
TOES; thrusting HIPS; crouched LEGS — makes it
hard to distinguish between the hoofing on the
stage and the boffing in the bedroom.

1920s' Chicago

Most of the scenes in *Chicago* are interiors (the theater, the prison, and the courthouse), but in a few key shots, such as Roxie's street and the finale at the Chicago Theater, there are views of the Windy City.

And how do you create 1920s Chicago when you're filming in Toronto? With special effects, of course. But, in truth, you'd have to use some special effects even if you were filming in Chicago, because so much of the city has changed over the decades. Here's how the filmmakers created the street where Roxie lives.

Beginning with an artist's concept of Roxie's neighborhood—a cobblestone street with the El in the background—the filmmakers found a quaint, down-at-the-heels street in east Toronto with small shops that would serve as the raw architecture of Roxie's street. Then, Raymond Gieringer, visual effects supervisor of Toronto special effects house Toybox, flew to Chicago where, with a location scout and photographer, he documented period buildings and designs to be used as texture maps and reference.

"Then we found an area in Toronto that had a nice cobblestone street where we shot period cars, extras in period dress, and the actors looking down this street that didn't exist yet," Gieringer says. "We kept the road, the cars, and the people and replaced everything else behind them with visual effects. From the ground level on up to the skyline, we added buildings and water towers and streetlamps, the El train and the El train tracks, and ultimately the landmark buildings in the background."

Using 3-D programs to create the buildings and matte painting to add texture, color and design, tucking the famous Wrigley and Tribune buildings into the background, then mixing in a little mist and fog for mood, the Toybox compositors ultimately created a completely convincing Chicago street scene, circa 1929.

BACKGROUND: Concept illustration for El train exterior shot.
RIGHT: Special effects plate (near right) and the final composite image (far right) from the movie.

There's a commotion at the back of the theater as Chicago POLICEMEN file in.

> **VELMA** (CONT'D)
> START THE CAR
> I KNOW A WHOOPEE SPOT
> WHERE THE GIN IS COLD
> BUT THE PIANO'S HOT
>
> **ENSEMBLE**
> SHOW HER WHERE TO PARK HER GIRDLE
> OH, HER MOTHER'S BLOOD'D CURDLE

Velma notices the cops moving in her direction. A defiant smile plays on her lips.

> **VELMA** (CONT'D)
> IT'S JUST A NOISY HALL
> WHERE THERE'S A NIGHTLY BRAWL
> AND ALL THAT JAZZ!
>
> **ENSEMBLE**
> IF SHE'D HEAR
> HER BABY'S QUEER
> FOR ALL THAT JAZZ!

Roxie whispers in Fred's ear, dreamily.

> **ROXIE**
> Say it again, Fred.
>
> **CASELY**
> You're a star, kid.
> (he's about to get off)
> My little shootin' star.

Roxie's hands reach up and grab the posts of the iron bed....

" One artist who really influenced our look was the French photographer Brassaï. In the 1930s, he did a whole series of photographs of Paris at night—cobbled streets lit by a single streetlight or chorus girls backstage. That was inspirational: Secret glimpses of everyday life in these little theaters. Although he always shot in black and white, his lighting was also very influential. He did some beautiful cityscapes, where the foregrounds are almost overexposed with the white light of bulbs, of electric signs, and the midgrounds are medium grays, and the backgrounds are charcoal grays melding into a black sky."

Brassaï, 1899-1984

—John Myhre, Production Designer

Left: "Blvd. de Clichy near the Gaumont Cinema," by Brassaï, 1933.

...as Velma grabs two guys by the wrists. They pull her on top of the piano.

> **VELMA**
> NO, I'M NO ONE'S WIFE
> BUT, OH, I LOVE MY LIFE
> AND ALL THAT JAZZ!
> THAT JAZZ!

Fred Casely climaxes. Roxie gasps. Velma sees the cops pouring into the wings. And the stage GOES BLACK.

INT. ROXIE'S APARTMENT - BEDROOM - NIGHT (ONE MONTH LATER)

In the darkness, a satisfied sigh from Fred Casely.

> **ROXIE** (V.O.)
> Say it again, Fred.

It's a month later, which means Casely doesn't bother answering anymore. Roxie tugs on the overhead light, sees him already pulling on his trousers.

> **ROXIE** (CONT'D)
> Hey, where's the fire? Amos ain't due home 'til midnight.

Casely grabs his clothes and disappears into the john. Roxie slips into a sad silk robe.

> **ROXIE** (CONT'D)
> Freddy...hon...now I don't want you to feel like I'm naggin' at you...

Casely pees, noisily. Roxie moves over to the Victrola and cranks it. Some heavy, rhythmic jazz.

> **ROXIE** (CONT'D)
> ...but don't you think it's about time I met your friend down at the Onyx? I mean, it's been almost a month since you told him about me.

The flush of the toilet is her only response.

> **ROXIE** (CONT'D)
> And I know 'cause that was the night Velma Kelly plugged her sister and her husband.

She picks up the morning *Tribune*. The headline reads: BILLY FLYNN TO DEFEND JAZZ SLAYER. There's a photo of Velma Kelly (taken the night she was arrested at the club) as well as a head shot of her dashing attorney, Billy Flynn. A smaller headline reads: KELLY CLAIMS TEMPORARY AMNESIA.

Roxie takes a seat at a large vanity dresser, an island of glamour in a sea of grey.

> **ROXIE** (CONT'D)
> They say she found 'em in the kip together. Geeps, if I ever found Amos slippin' it to someone else, I'd throw him a party.

She applies some lipstick, her mouth exaggerated in the make-up mirror.

> **ROXIE** (CONT'D)
> A great big goin' away party.

Casely emerges from the bathroom, buttoning his shirt.

> **CASELY**
> It's gettin' late.

Roxie jumps up. Anything to keep him there a little longer.

> **ROXIE**
> I been thinkin' a lot about my act. See, whenever I get a good idea, I try to write it down before it goes out of my head.

She unlocks a silver diary with a frilly "ROXIE" drawn on the cover, the "I" dotted with a heart.

> **ROXIE** (CONT'D) (READING)
> Oh, right. It hit me the other day that all the really knockout acts have somethin' a little different goin' on. You know, a signature bit.

She drops the diary and dances suggestively in front of Casely.

> **ROXIE** (CONT'D)
> I thought my thing could be...aloof.

She grabs Casely's tie, plays with it.

> **ROXIE** (CONT'D)
> Give 'em enough to get 'em good and hungry, but always leave 'em wanting more.

She tugs on the tie. Casely swats her away.

> **ROXIE** (CONT'D)
> And once I get a name for myself, maybe we can open a club of our own. You can run it and I'll be the headliner.

She reaches down to kiss him. Casely pushes her this time, hard enough to send her stumbling into the wall.

Renée Zellweger

"I love this character," Renée Zellweger says of Roxie Hart, the jazz gal who kills her boyfriend and then tries to parlay her newfound notoriety into a stage career. "She's so earnest in a way, and tragic. She's so desperate for fame because of what she thinks it will bring: Self-esteem, self-respect, self-worth, love...all the things that she doesn't have a lot of. She's doing the best she knows how. And the sad reality is that, as we all know, it's a fallacy."

Zellweger confesses to being intimidated by her costars Catherine Zeta-Jones and Richard Gere, because, unlike them, she had little experience singing and dancing. When she arrived for the intensive rehearsals, Zellweger saw Zeta-Jones practicing the film's opening number "All That Jazz." "I just went, Oh my gosh, what have I done? I have some catching up to do."

And where was she starting from? "We watched *The Sound of Music* every year on TV, and my father had the soundtrack," Zellweger says. "That was the extent of my experience. I didn't really grow up around musical theater or have any reason to sing except in the shower, with my brother down the hall screaming, 'Please shut up.'

"I mean Catherine has been doing this since she was a little girl. This is where she started so she's in her element here. She's so powerful as a singer and a dancer, you are blown away. She has this vivacity, this grand energy that elevates the energy in any room she enters."

And then there was her other costar, Gere, who had also performed in musicals. "We were rehearsing for the song 'We Both Reached for the Gun.' Richard sat down at the piano, and he just started playing, and I thought, 'Oh my God. He sings, tap dances, does all this other stuff, fantastic actor, not hard to look at, *and he plays piano.*'"

Of course, Zellweger turned out to be a genuinely gifted singer herself; she just hadn't trained professionally. The six weeks of rehearsals helped to bring out her inner hoofer. And she was changed forever by the experience. "It was fantastically liberating. It was one of those life-enhancing, life-changing experiences, learning to express myself in a different way, discovering a new way to emote. It was unbelievable. It was magical," Zellweger says.

But while it was exhilarating, it was also hard work—week after week of training and practice, like school or boot camp. What was the hardest part? "Coming down the stairs with your head up in high heel shoes. Woo, ha! It's a lot trickier than it looks."

ROXIE (CONT'D)
Hey. What's the idea?

CASELY
Wake up, kiddo. You ain't never gonna have an act.

ROXIE
Says who?

CASELY
Face it, Roxie. You're a two-bit talent with skinny legs. And I'm just a furniture salesman.

ROXIE
Well sure, but you got connections. That guy down at the club...

CASELY
There is no guy.

ROXIE
But that night...

CASELY
...was the first time I set foot in that joint. I was collectin' on a bet from the trombone player.

Roxie gets strangely quiet as the truth seeps in.

ROXIE
So you never told anyone about me?

CASELY
Sugar, you were hot stuff. I woulda said anything to get some of that.

ROXIE
And now?

CASELY
We had some laughs.

He reaches for his fedora.

CASELY (CONT'D)
Let's leave it at that.

ROXIE
Fred, you can't do this to me....

She throws her arms around him, desperate. The more he tries to pull away, the harder she holds on. Finally he curls his fingers and smashes her in the mouth.

Roxie crumples against the bureau. Casely looms over her.

CASELY
Touch me again and I'll put your lights out.

Casely adjusts his hat in the mirror. Roxie slides open the bottom drawer.

CASELY (CONT'D)
Your husband'll be home soon. Why don't you wash yourself before you go spreadin' those legs again?

Roxie's fingers feel for something hidden under Amos' boxer shorts.

ROXIE
You're a liar, Fred. You lied to me.

CASELY
That's life, sweetheart.

ROXIE
You son-of-a-bitch!

She aims a snub-nosed revolver at Casely and shoots.

CASELY (A LOOK OF SURPRISE)
Shit.

Casely falls. She shoots him two more times and he dies.

Roxie catches her reflection in the mirror, her face framed by make-up lights.

INT. THE ONYX - NIGHT
The chorines undulate across the stage.

ENSEMBLE
JAZZ...

ENSEMBLE (CONT'D)
WHOOPEE...

ENSEMBLE (CONT'D)
HOTCHA!

INT. ROXIE'S APARTMENT - BEDROOM - NIGHT
Roxie drops the gun and stares into the mirror, bewildered and suddenly frightened. We FADE OUT.

INT. ROXIE'S APARTMENT - BEDROOM - NIGHT (LATER)
A police PHOTOGRAPHER takes a picture of the corpse, while a FORENSICS MAN dusts the mirror for fingerprints.

PHOTOGRAPHER
Why you botherin', Sal? This one's all wrapped up.

The photographer straddles the body, leans down for a close shot of Casely's startled expression.

PHOTOGRAPHER (CONT'D)
I hear it's a new city record. From killing to confession in an hour flat.

He drops the sheet back over Casely's face. We move with him through a gridlock of cops to the parlor, where Sgt. FOGARTY is taking down a statement.

SGT. FOGARTY
...and where'd you get the murder weapon?

Roxie turns to her husband AMOS, who stares at his grime-covered hands. With his weak chin and receding hairline, Amos is so unassuming that he almost seems invisible.

AMOS
I keep a gun in the underwear drawer. Just in case of trouble, you know...

SGT. FOGARTY (FINISHING WRITING)
Well that's just fine. Sign right there, Mr. Hart.

So he's the one who's confessing...

AMOS
I gave myself up. Surrendered of my own free will.

[Assistant District Attorney MARTIN HARRISON enters. He grabs Amos by the collar.]

HARRISON (CONT'D)
Get in there.

He pushes Amos into the bedroom, turns to Roxie.

HARRISON (CONT'D)
You, too.

Harrison grabs a flashlight from Sgt. Fogarty.

INT. ROXIE'S APARTMENT - BEDROOM - NIGHT
Roxie has to step over the corpse to enter the room. Harrison pushes Amos into a wooden chair, points Roxie to a spot on the bed behind him. She gazes at the freshly soiled sheets and decides to lean against the bureau instead. She nervously lights a cigarette.

Harrison shines the flashlight in Amos's face.

What if the world
Slandered my name?
Why, he'd be right there
Taking the blame
He loves me so
And it all suits me fine
That funny, sunny, honey
Hubby of mine!

HARRISON
Okay, from the top.

AMOS
A man's got a right to protect his home and his loved ones, right?

HARRISON
Of course he has.

[Amos claims that when he got home from work he saw the man coming through the window.]

HARRISON
Uh-huh.

Roxie nonchalantly reaches down and turns the wedding picture right side up.

AMOS
With my wife Roxie layin' there, sleepin' like an angel…an angel!

Harrison shines the harsh light in Roxie's face.

HARRISON
Is that true, Mrs. Hart?

Roxie squints in the glare, doesn't answer. Her eyes dart around, looking for a way to escape.

AMOS (O.C.)
I'm telling you, it's the God's honest truth. My wife had nothin' to do with it. She wouldn't hurt a worm. Not even a worm.

Moving in on Roxie. A look of gratitude mixing in with the fear now.

INT. "STAGE" - NIGHT
The light shining on Roxie's face broadens into a stage spot.

AMOS (O.C.)
It wasn't until I fired the first shot she even opened her eyes. Boy, is she some heavy sleeper. I always said, she could sleep through the St. Paddy's Day Parade….

Amos's voice starts to fade away, replaced by the bandleader:

BANDLEADER (O.C.)
For her first number, Miss Roxie Hart would like to sing a song of love and devotion dedicated to her dear husband Amos…

ROXIE (CIGARETTE IN HAND)
SOMETIMES I'M RIGHT

SOMETIMES I'M WRONG
BUT HE DOESN'T CARE
HE'LL STRING ALONG
HE LOVES ME SO
THAT FUNNY HONEY OF MINE!

Roxie sings the torch song leaning against the piano, à la Helen Morgan. It's as if the only way for her to deal with this terrifying situation is to transport herself to the world she's always dreamed about — to see her life as a vaudeville act.

ROXIE (CONT'D)
SOMETIMES I'M DOWN
SOMETIMES I'M UP
BUT HE FOLLOWS 'ROUND
LIKE SOME DROOPY-EYED PUP
HE LOVES ME SO
THAT FUNNY HONEY OF MINE

INT. ROXIE'S APARTMENT - BEDROOM - NIGHT
Amos seems to be enjoying the attention he's receiving.

AMOS
…like I said, even after I shot him he kept comin' at me. So I had to pull the trigger again.

He wipes his nose with his dirty shirtsleeve.

INT. "STAGE" - NIGHT
Roxie climbs onto the upright.

ROXIE
HE AIN'T NO SHEIK
THAT'S NO GREAT PHYSIQUE
LORD KNOWS, HE AIN'T GOT THE SMARTS
BUT LOOK AT THAT SOUL
I TELL YOU, THAT WHOLE
IS A WHOLE LOT GREATER
THAN THE SUM OF HIS PARTS
AND IF YOU KNEW HIM LIKE ME
I KNOW YOU'D AGREE

Roxie lounges sexily on the piano.

ROXIE (CONT'D)
WHAT IF THE WORLD
SLANDERED MY NAME?
WHY, HE'D BE RIGHT THERE
TAKING THE BLAME
HE LOVES ME SO
AND IT ALL SUITS ME FINE
THAT FUNNY, SUNNY, HONEY
HUBBY OF MINE!

INT. ROXIE'S APARTMENT - BEDROOM - NIGHT
A detective slips a wallet to Harrison.

> **AMOS**
>
> I mean supposin', just supposin', he had violated her or somethin'…you know what I mean…violated?

> **HARRISON**
>
> I know what you mean.

> **AMOS**
>
> …or somethin'. Think how terrible that would have been. Good thing I got home from work on time, I'm tellin' ya that! I say I'm tellin' you that!

INT. "STAGE" - NIGHT
Roxie thrusts her hips and legs in the air.

> **ROXIE**
>
> HE LOVES ME SO
> THAT FUNNY HONEY OF MINE!

INT. ROXIE'S APARTMENT - NIGHT
Harrison opens the wallet.

> **HARRISON**
>
> Name of deceased. Fred Casely.

> **AMOS**
>
> Fred Casely? How could he be a burglar? My wife knows him! He sold us our furniture!

INT. "STAGE" - NIGHT
Roxie frowns, starting to smell trouble.

> **AMOS** (V.O.)
>
> He gave us ten percent off!

> **ROXIE**
>
> LORD KNOWS, HE AIN'T GOT THE SMARTS

INT. ROXIE'S APARTMENT - NIGHT
Amos looks betrayed and hurt.

> **AMOS**
>
> You told me he was a burglar.

> **HARRISON**
>
> You mean he was dead when you got home?

> **AMOS**
>
> She had him covered with a sheet and she's tellin' me some cock-and-bull story about this burglar, and I ought to say I did it 'cause I was sure to get off. Help me, Amos, she says. It's my goddamn hour of need.

All eyes are on Roxie now.

He
loves me
so...

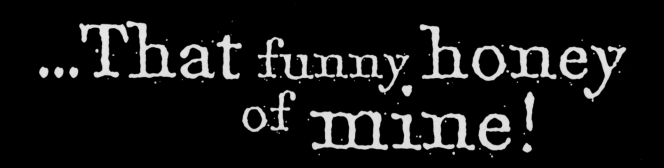

...That funny honey of mine!

INT. "STAGE" - NIGHT

Amos is now sitting in a wooden chair, bathed in his own spotlight. Roxie looms over him on the piano.

ROXIE
NOW, HE'S SHOT OFF HIS TRAP
I CAN'T STAND THAT SAP
LOOK AT HIM GO
RATTIN' ON ME
WITH JUST ONE MORE BRAIN
WHAT A HALF-WIT HE'D BE
IF THEY STRING ME UP
I'LL KNOW WHO BROUGHT THE TWINE
THAT SCUMMY, CRUMMY, DUMMY
HUBBY OF MINE!?

AMOS
And I believed her! That cheap little tramp. So, she was two-timin' me, huh? Well I'm through with protectin' her now. She can swing for all I care. Boy, I'm down at the garage, working my butt off 14 hours a day, and she's up here munchin' on bonbons and trampin' around like some goddamn floozie. Thought she could pull the wool over my eyes. Huh! I wasn't born yesterday. I'm telling you, there's certain things a man just can't accept, and this time she pushed me too far. That little chiseler. Boy, what a sap I was!

Roxie climbs off the piano and marches over to Amos. She pushes his chair over with her foot.

INT. ROXIE'S APARTMENT - NIGHT

Roxie explodes in rage.

ROXIE
You double crosser! You big blabber mouth.

AMOS
You told me he was a burglar and all the while you're up here jazzing him.

ROXIE
Goddamn you! You are a disloyal husband.

A direct appeal to Harrison:

ROXIE (CONT'D)
Look, it's true, I shot him. But it was self defense. He was trying to burgle me.

HARRISON
From what I hear, he's been burgling you three times a week for the last month.

Harrison nods to the detective, who brings in the neighbor, Mrs. Borusewicz. He lifts the sheet covering Casely's face. The dour woman enjoys her moment in the spotlight.

HARRISON (CONT'D)
So what do you say, Missus?

MRS. BORUSEWICZ
That's him all right.

HARRISON
Thank you.

The woman is led out. Harrison leans into Roxie with the flashlight.

[He holds open the wallet. A small family photo is inside.]

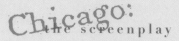

HARRISON (CONT'D)
[He had] a wife and five little Caselys.

Roxie is steaming, but tries to keep a lid on it.

HARRISON (CONT'D)
Or did he forget to mention them?

Harrison lets out a loud cackle. That cuts it. Roxie knocks aside the flashlight.

ROXIE
That bastard.

[She confesses to killing Casely.]

He turns stiffly to the detective.

HARRISON (CONT'D)
Get her out of here.

EXT. ROXIE'S APARTMENT BUILDING - NIGHT
A small crowd watches Roxie being led out in hand-cuffs. A car pulls up and a REPORTER and PHO-TOGRAPHER jump out.

NEWSPAPER PHOTOGRAPHER
This way, lady!

Roxie covers her face with her cuffed hands.

NEWSPAPER PHOTOGRAPHER (CONT'D)
Aw, c'mon. It's a shame to hide a pretty face like that.

Roxie lowers her hands, squints as the flashbulb pops. The REPORTER falls into step next to her.

REPORTER
Why'd you shoot him, hon?

[Roxie is too rattled to answer. Harrison grabs her by the elbow.]

HARRISON
Enjoy it while you can.

He tosses her into the back of a paddy wagon.

Roxie lifts her cuffed hands and starts to pray.

HARRISON
Not so tough anymore, are you?

ROXIE
Hail Mary, full of grace, the Lord is with thee. Blessed art thou amongst women...

HARRISON
Take her down to the Cook County Jail.

Roxie sits alone, trembling, as the doors are slammed shut. The paddy wagon starts off, with the photographer trotting behind.

EXT. COOK COUNTY JAIL - WOMEN'S WARD - PRE-DAWN
The soft glow of a winter night, just before sunrise. The paddy wagon enters the inner city prison, an oppressive stone compound. An American flag flaps lazily in the breeze. SHARPSHOOTERS stand on the parapets.

INT. COOK COUNTY JAIL - WOMEN'S WARD - DAY
Roxie stands opposite a prison CLERK.

CLERK'S VOICE
Use morphine? Opium? Cocaine?

Roxie shakes her head no.

INT. COOK COUNTY JAIL - WOMEN'S WARD - DAY
Roxie stands in front of a measuring wall, her back to us, naked to the waist.

INT. COOK COUNTY JAIL - HOLDING ROOM - NIGHT (LATER)
Roxie and several new INMATES are led into a small room. They each hold a blanket, a towel, and a bar of soap.

GUARD
The matron's on her way, so don't get too cozy. And put out that cigarette.

He leaves. NICKIE, a hooker with a heart of lead, ignores the order.

NICKIE
Ever had Morton before?

Roxie looks down, shakes her head.

NICKIE (CONT'D)
She's fine, long as you keep her happy.

She rubs an invisible dollar through her fingers. Roxie moves away, taking a seat in back.

INT. COOK COUNTY JAIL - HALLWAY - NIGHT
We MOVE in front of the MATRON, whom we see from the neck down, badge bobbing on her chest.

INT. COOK COUNTY JAIL - HOLDING ROOM - NIGHT
Roxie sees the matron's shadow through a frosted glass wall.

BANDLEADER (V.O.)
And now, ladies and gentlemen — the Keeper of the Keys, the Countess of

Chita Rivera

Winner of two Tony Awards for Best Actress in a Musical and the first Hispanic American to receive the Kennedy Center Honors, Chita Rivera is synonymous with the Broadway musical. Rivera made her Broadway debut in the chorus of *Call Me Madam* in 1952, and then she went on to become the first Anita in *West Side Story*, and, of course, the first Velma in *Chicago*.

Now 70, Rivera returned to the scene of the crime by agreeing to play Nickie, "a hooker with a heart of lead," in the movie version of *Chicago*.

"It was so great to have Chita in our company," says director Rob Marshall, "because she was so brilliant as the original Velma Kelly. I felt like it was her stamp of approval of this production and what we'd done with it. It was nice to carry the lineage of that. I've worked with Chita a lot—I've choreographed her, and directed her—so it was very special having her there."

Got a little **motto** Always sees me through When you're **good to mama** Mama's good to you There's a lot of **favors** I'm prepared **to do** You do one for mama She'll do one **for you**

the Clink, the Mistress of Murderer's Row —
Matron Mama Morton!

Roxie shrinks into herself as the doorknob starts
to turn. The door opens in a blast of white light,
which becomes...

INT. "STAGE" - NIGHT

...the coy fluttering of a WHITE FEATHER FAN.
MATRON "MAMA" MORTON steps out from behind
the fan. Middle-aged, heavyset, she wears a rhinestone badge on her chest.

> **MATRON**
> ASK ANY OF THE CHICKIES IN MY PEN
> THEY'LL TELL YOU I'M THE BIGGEST
>   MOTHER HEN
> I LOVE THEM ALL AND ALL OF THEM LOVE ME
> BECAUSE THE SYSTEM WORKS
> THE SYSTEM CALLED RECIPROCITY...

Mama does a saucy bump-and-grind across the stage.

> **MATRON** (CONT'D)
> GOT A LITTLE MOTTO
> ALWAYS SEES ME THROUGH
> WHEN YOU'RE GOOD TO MAMA
> MAMA'S GOOD TO YOU
> THERE'S A LOT OF FAVORS
> I'M PREPARED TO DO
> YOU DO ONE FOR MAMA
> SHE'LL DO ONE FOR YOU

The matron moves through the audience, teasing
them with the fan. She flirts with a MALE CUS-
TOMER, then the WOMAN next to him.

> **MATRON** (CONT'D)
> THEY SAY THAT LIFE IS TIT FOR TAT
> AND THAT'S THE WAY I LIVE
> SO I DESERVE A LOT OF TAT
> FOR WHAT I'VE GOT TO GIVE
> DON'T YOU KNOW THAT THIS HAND
> WASHES THAT ONE TOO
> WHEN YOU'RE GOOD TO MAMA
> MAMA'S GOOD TO YOU!

Mama moves behind one of the scrim panels. As
she dances in silhouette:

INT. COOK COUNTY JAIL - HOLDING ROOM - NIGHT (LATER)
The door opens, for real this time. The guard enters.

> **GUARD**
> On your feet.

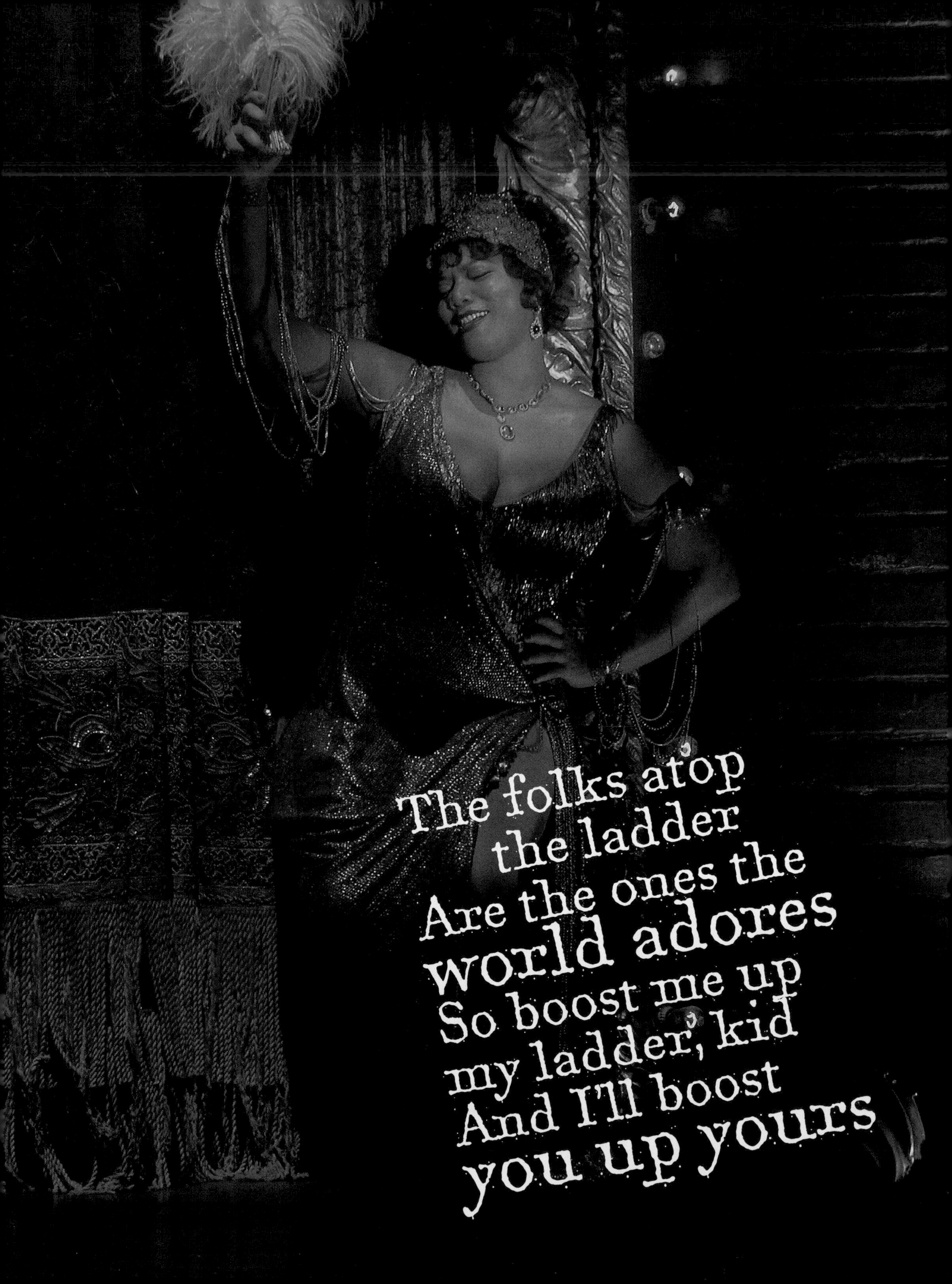

The folks atop
the ladder
Are the ones the
world adores
So boost me up
my ladder, kid
And I'll boost
you up yours

The women stand. The matron enters, fixes them with a kind smile.

>**MATRON**
>Welcome, ladies. You might think I'm here to make your life a livin' hell, but that's just not true.

She walks down the line of new inmates.

>**MATRON** (CONT'D)
>I'd like to be your friend, if you let me. So if there's something that upsets you, or makes you unhappy in any way...

She stops at the end of the line, turns back to the women.

>**MATRON** (CONT'D)
>Don't shoot your fat ass mouth off to me 'cause I don't give a shit.

Roxie's face falls.

>**MATRON** (CONT'D)
>Now move it out.

The women file out the door. The matron steps in front of Roxie.

>**MATRON** (CONT'D)
>You must be Hart.

Roxie nods nervously.

>**MATRON** (CONT'D)
>Ain't you the pretty one.

>**ROXIE**
>Thank you, ma'am.

>**MATRON**
>Call me Mama. I'm here to take care of you.

She brushes her fingers along Roxie's hand.

>**MATRON** (CONT'D)
>You'll be habitating down in the East Block. Murderess Row, we call it.

>**ROXIE** (EVER HOPEFUL)
>Oh...is that nicer?

The matron smiles, holds the door open for Roxie.

INT. COOK COUNTY JAIL - HALLWAY - NIGHT
The guard escorts Roxie, with the matron hanging a few steps behind.

Queen Latifah

Rapper, singer, and actress, Queen Latifah would seem to have done it all. But one thing she hadn't done was perform in a musical—not counting high school productions. As for merging all of her talents in the film, she just shrugs and laughs, "Well, I have a few more talents I didn't use in the film."

It's that lusty sense of fun that comes across in her Sophie Tucker-inspired rendition of the song "When You're Good to Mama," which sums up the philosophy of her character, the prison matron Mama Morton: "When you're good to Mama/Mama's good to you."

"Mama is mama in more ways than one," Latifah says. "She is definitely the queen of the castle when it comes to that prison. If you need anything, you gotta go through Mama. It's all about reciprocity with Mama. Mama's lookin' to make a buck. That's why in the song, Mama sings, 'If you want my gravy/Pepper my ragout/Spice it up for Mama/She'll get hot for you.' She's kinda tough, but she gets what she wants."

ROXIE (TURNING)
I don't really belong in here. See I didn't actually do anything wrong...

VELMA (O.S.)
Hey Mama!

Velma Kelly approaches, holding up a magazine. She is wearing a red kimono, over silk lounging pajamas.

ROXIE
Oh my God, Velma Kelly. You're the Velma Kelly.

Velma is flattered, but doesn't dare show it.

ROXIE (CONT'D)
You know, I was there the night you got arrested.

VELMA
Yeah, you and half of Chicago.

Velma ignores her, turns to the matron.

VELMA (CONT'D)
Look at this, Mama. There's an editorial denouncing me in *Redbook* magazine.
(reading)
"Not in memory do we recall so fiendish and horrible a double homicide."

MUSIC starts under:

MATRON
Ah, baby, you couldn't buy that kind of publicity.

VELMA
Couldn't buy it? I guess I can keep this then.

She holds up a folded wad of bills. The matron grabs the money, tucks it into her cleavage, and smiles.

MATRON
Nice try.

INT. "STAGE" - NIGHT
The matron pulls a green scarf from her bosom, Sophie Tucker-style.

MATRON
IF YOU WANT MY GRAVY
PEPPER MY RAGOUT
SPICE IT UP FOR MAMA
SHE'LL GET HOT FOR YOU

INT. COOK COUNTY JAIL - CELLBLOCK - NIGHT
The matron leads Roxie onto Murderess Row, two stories of tiny cages filled with hardened criminals. Roxie stares at the faces, haunted, worn, old before their time.

As they pass one cell, a sexy inmate (ANNIE) adjusts her stocking, offering a flash of thigh.

MATRON (V.O.)
WHEN THEY PASS THAT BASKET
FOLKS CONTRIBUTE TO
YOU PUT IN FOR MAMA
SHE'LL PUT OUT FOR YOU

The matron slips a pack of cigarettes into Annie's stocking, gives her thigh a playful slap.

INT. "STAGE" - NIGHT
The matron runs the scarf across her behind.

MATRON
THE FOLKS ATOP THE LADDER
ARE THE ONES THE WORLD ADORES
SO BOOST ME UP MY LADDER, KID
AND I'LL BOOST YOU UP YOURS

INT. COOK COUNTY JAIL - NIGHT
Roxie moves down the cell block, fighting back tears.

MATRON (V.O.)
LET'S ALL STROKE TOGETHER
LIKE THE PRINCETON CREW
WHEN YOU'RE STROKIN' MAMA
MAMA'S STROKIN' YOU

INT. "STAGE" - NIGHT
The matron stands center stage, a little winded.

MATRON
SO WHAT'S THE ONE CONCLUSION
I CAN BRING THIS NUMBER TO?
WHEN YOU'RE GOOD TO MAMA
MAMA'S GOOD TO YOU!

A final smash of the drums, as we CUT TO:

INT. COOK COUNTY JAIL - NIGHT
The matron slams the cell door on Roxie, to the shrill blast of a siren.

ROXIE
Um, Mama...

The matron stops. Already put out.

ROXIE (CONT'D)
It's a little, you know...freezing in here.
Do you think maybe there's a problem
with the heating system?

The matron just stares.

ROXIE (CONT'D)
Not that I'm complaining, mind you. But if you
got a few extra blankets tucked away...

The guard smashes a billy club against the metal
bars. Roxie jumps back in terror. The matron and
the guard move off.

MATRON
Lights out, ladies.

Another GUARD turns a massive BRASS WHEEL,
which locks down the cells for the night.

INT. ROXIE'S CELL - NIGHT (LATER)
Roxie lies awake on her cot. She stares at a
leaky faucet, dripping relentlessly. She tries to
ignore the sounds coming from other cells. The
ticking of a clock. The tapping of a guard's shoe
on the catwalk. The drumming of fingernails on
a bed frame.

The dripping, tapping, ticking and drumming all
join in percussive rhythm in Roxie's brain.

INT. COOK COUNTY JAIL - CELL BLOCK - NIGHT
One woman (LIZ) strikes a match in the darkness.

LIZ
POP.

Another (ANNIE) curls her fingers around a
prison bar.

ANNIE
SIX.

A third woman (JUNE) flattens a cockroach with
her foot.

JUNE
SQUISH.

Another inmate (HUNYAK) clutches a pair of rosary beads.

> **HUNYAK**
> UH UH.

The glow of a cigarette in another cell. (VELMA)

> **VELMA**
> CICERO.

A sixth woman (MONA) cracks her knuckles.

> **MONA**
> LIPSCHITZ.

INT. ROXIE'S CELL - NIGHT

Roxie glances up. Her cell bars slide open and keep SLIDING...

INT. "STAGE" - NIGHT

...an endless roll of steel. Behind them, the blurred image of the bandleader, in a pin spot.

> **BANDLEADER**
> And now, the six merry murderesses of the Cook County jail in their rendition of the Cell Block Tango.

The bars clang to a stop. Roxie stands and steps into the club. She takes a seat at a center table, an audience of one. On the stage, the six inmates stand behind a set of bars.

> **LIZ**
> POP.

> **ANNIE**
> SIX.

> **JUNE**
> SQUISH.

> **HUNYAK**
> UH UH.

> **VELMA**
> CICERO.

> **MONA**
> LIPSCHITZ.

MUSIC starts under.

> **LIZ**
> POP.

> **ANNIE**
> SIX.

JUNE
SQUISH.

HUNYAK
UH UH.

VELMA
CICERO.

MONA
LIPSCHITZ.

Now the rhythm is heavy and insistent.

LIZ
POP.

ANNIE
SIX.

JUNE
SQUISH.

HUNYAK
UH UH.

VELMA
CICERO.

MONA
LIPSCHITZ.

The cell bars light up, outlined in neon.

ALL
HE HAD IT COMING
HE HAD IT COMING
HE ONLY HAD HIMSELF TO BLAME
IF YOU'D HAVE BEEN THERE
IF YOU'D HAVE SEEN IT

VELMA
I BETCHA YOU WOULD HAVE DONE THE SAME!

LIZ
POP.

ANNIE
SIX.

JUNE
SQUISH.

HUNYAK
UH UH.

VELMA
CICERO.

MONA
LIPSCHITZ.

One set of bars descends into the stage floor and LIZ steps forward. At the same time, a MALE FIGURE rises into view.

LIZ
You know how people have these little habits that get you down? Like Bernie. Bernie liked to chew gum. No, not chew. POP. I came home this one day and I am really irritated, and looking for a little sympathy and there's Bernie layin' on the couch, drinkin' a beer and chewin'.

EXT. COOK COUNTY JAIL - CELL BLOCK - NIGHT
The inmates file down the catwalks in military formation, all to the strict accompaniment of a guard's whistle. Roxie walks next to Liz, who mutters under her breath, to no one in particular. Behind them, a sign reads: SILENCE.

LIZ
No, not chewin'. Poppin'. So I said to him, "You pop that gum one more time…"

Roxie avoids the unstable woman's gaze.

INT. "STAGE" - NIGHT
Liz pushes her victim to the floor.

LIZ
And he did. So I took the shotgun off the wall and I fired two warning shots…into his head.

Liz pulls a red scarf from under her victim's hat and kicks him across the stage. Behind her, the other prisoners stomp and point.

ALL
HE HAD IT COMING
HE HAD IT COMING
HE ONLY HAD HIMSELF TO BLAME
IF YOU'D HAVE BEEN THERE
IF YOU'D HAVE HEARD IT
I BETCHA YOU WOULD HAVE DONE THE SAME!

ANNIE, a throaty blonde, approaches another MALE FIGURE.

ANNIE
I met Ezekial Young from Salt Lake City about two years ago and he told me he was single and we hit it off right away. So, we started living together.

INT. COOK COUNTY JAIL - COMMON ROOM - ANOTHER NIGHT
Roxie sits alone, smoking and playing a game of

88

solitaire. At the next table, Velma runs a poker
game with a few old-timers, including Annie.
The pot includes cigarettes, buttons, even a
lipstick tube.

    ANNIE
    He'd go to work, he'd come home, I'd mix him
    a drink, we'd have dinner. And then I found
    out. Single, he told me?

A guard enters the room. The women hide their
cards and cover the pot with a newspaper.

INT. "STAGE" - NIGHT
Annie tangos with her partner.

    ANNIE
    Single, my ass. Not only was he married...oh,
    no, he had six wives. One of those Mormons,
    you know. So that night, when he came home, I
    mixed him his drink, as usual. You know, some
    guys just can't hold their arsenic.

She pulls a red scarf from her partner's mouth.
Behind her, the women climb onto the bars.

    LIZ, ANNIE, JUNE, MONA
    HE HAD IT COMING
    HE HAD IT COMING
    HE TOOK A FLOWER IN ITS PRIME
    AND THEN HE USED IT
    AND HE ABUSED IT
    IT WAS A MURDER BUT NOT A CRIME

    GIRLS
    POP, SIX, SQUISH, UH UH,
    CICERO, LIPSCHITZ
    POP, SIX, SQUISH, UH UH,
    CICERO, LIPSCHITZ
    POP, SIX, SQUISH, UH UH,
    CICERO, LIPSCHITZ

JUNE emerges from her cell, faces off with another
MALE FIGURE.

    JUNE
    Now I'm standing in the kitchen carvin' up the
    chicken for dinner, minding my own business,
    and in storms my husband Wilbur in a jealous
    rage. "You been screwin' the milkman," he
    says. He was crazy and he kept screamin',
    "You been screwin' the milkman."

INT. COOK COUNTY JAIL - BATHROOM - ANOTHER NIGHT
June stares into a mirror, brushing her teeth. She

Costuming the Criminals

"The 'Cell Block Tango' costumes have a bondage vibe that was inspired by a black-and-white photograph from the '20s by the French artist Man Ray. It's of a woman with a black piece of elastic across her chest and over her privates and black high heels, and she has her hands bound. I was like, wow, this is it for that number. And I showed it to Rob, and he got really excited too.

"Then there is the innuendo with Mama and the girls. You know, women behind bars—that whole kind of sweaty, hot, stinking mess of all these women, half of whom have had very bad experiences with men. There is definitely the vibe of not necessarily women who go with women, but women who do whatever they want. And if they are hanging out together in the dorm, they might as well just wear their underwear. But you get girls like that, that are all pent up, you are going to get that sexuality thing going on.

"That scene made me smile, because it really was like some naughty novel. It's like those funny novels in Latin America with the picture of a girl on the cover with barely any clothes on, just sort of titillating. I played with that idea of what people think women do in prison. And Mama had to have something going on to keep her interested."

—COLLEEN ATWOOD, COSTUME DESIGNER

Blanc et noir variante, *1935 by Man Ray.*

93

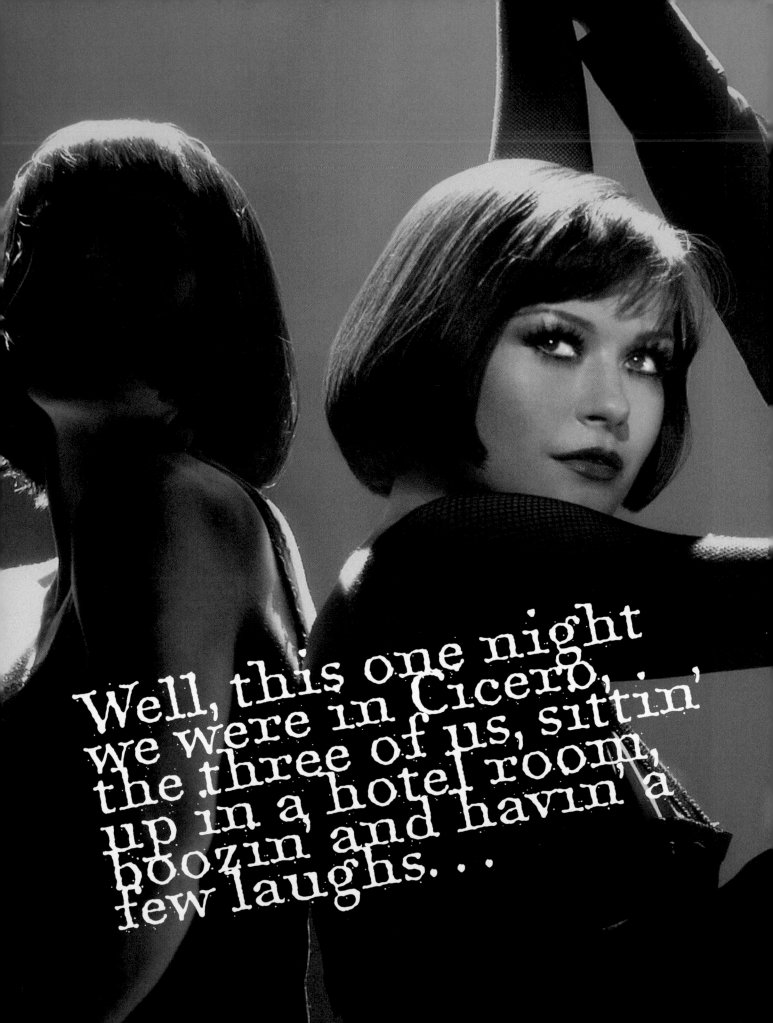

chats with Liz, while Roxie scrubs her face at the next sink.

JUNE
And then he ran into my knife.

Roxie turns. A little chilled.

JUNE (CONT'D)
He ran into my knife ten times.

INT. "STAGE" - NIGHT
June pulls a long scarf from her victim's stomach. She twists her way through the scarf.

ALL
IF YOU'D HAVE BEEN THERE
IF YOU'D HAVE SEEN IT
I BETCHA YOU WOULD HAVE DONE THE SAME!

KATALIN HALENSCKI — better known as the HUNYAK — steps forward. She does a sad romantic tango with her PARTNER.

HUNYAK (HUNGARIAN)
Mit keresek, en itt? Azt mondjok, hogy a hires lakem lefogta a ferjemet en meg leesaptam a fejet. De nem igaz, en artatlan vagyok. Nem tudom mert mondja Uncle Sam hogy en tettem.

INT. COOK COUNTY JAIL - HALLWAY - DAY
Roxie and the Hunyak scrub the floor on their hands and knees.

HUNYAK
Probaltam a rendorsegen megmagyaranzi de nem ertettek meg...

ROXIE
But did you do it?

INT. "STAGE" - NIGHT
A look of confusion and terror on the Hunyak's face.

HUNYAK
UH UH, not guilty!

She reaches behind her partner and pulls out a white scarf.

ALL (UNDER)
HE HAD IT COMING
HE HAD IT COMING
HE HAD IT COMING ALL ALONG

Velma is released from her cell. A MALE and FE-MALE FIGURE — Velma's husband, CHARLIE, and her sister, VERONICA — rise from the stage floor.

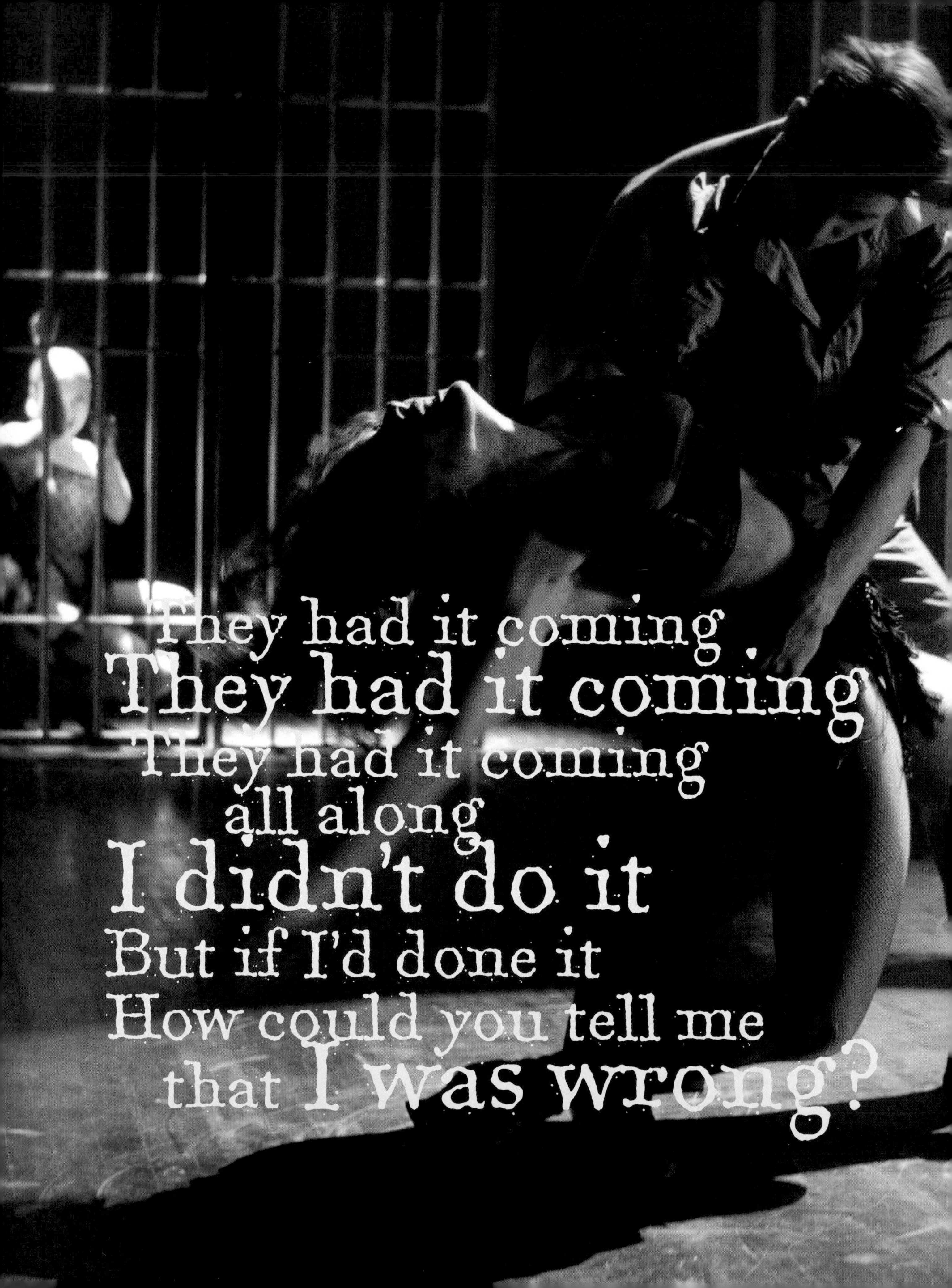

They had it coming
They had it coming
They had it coming
all along
I didn't do it
But if I'd done it
How could you tell me
that I was wrong?

VELMA

My sister, Veronica, and I did this double act and my husband, Charlie, traveled around with us. Now, for the last number in our act, we did these twenty acrobatic tricks in a row, one, two, three, four, five...splits, spread eagles, flip flops, back flips, one right after the other.

INT. COOK COUNTY JAIL - CELL BLOCK - ANOTHER DAY

A GUARD leads a line of inmates, including Roxie, down the cell block. They pass Velma's cell, where a newspaper PHOTOGRAPHER is snapping pictures of Velma surrounded by flowers and gifts and fan mail. She is giving an interview to a REPORTER.

VELMA

So this one night before the show, we're down at the Hotel Cicero, the three of us boozin' and havin' a few laughs, and we ran out of ice. So I went out to get some.

It's more like a showbiz anecdote than a murder confession, and the reporter is hanging on every word.

INT. "STAGE" - NIGHT

Veronica rides Charlie, her crotch in his face.

VELMA

...I come back, open the door, and there's Veronica and Charlie doing Number Seventeen — the spread eagle. Well, I was in such a state of shock, I completely blacked out. I can't remember a thing. It wasn't until later when I was washin' the blood off my hands I even knew they were dead.

Velma pulls out two scarves, one from each victim.

VELMA (CONT'D)
THEY HAD IT COMING
THEY HAD IT COMING
THEY HAD IT COMING ALL ALONG
I DIDN'T DO IT
BUT IF I'D DONE IT
HOW COULD YOU TELL ME THAT I WAS WRONG?

The women pound the floor with their feet.

VELMA (CONT'D)
THEY HAD IT COMING
THEY HAD IT COMING
THEY HAD IT COMING ALL ALONG
I DIDN'T DO IT

BUT IF I'D DONE IT
HOW COULD YOU TELL ME THAT I WAS WRONG?

GIRLS
THEY HAD IT COMING
THEY HAD IT COMING
THEY TOOK A FLOWER IN ITS PRIME
AND THEN THEY USED IT
AND THEY ABUSED IT
IT WAS A MURDER BUT NOT A CRIME

MONA, barely twenty, steps forward.

MONA
I loved Al Lipschitz more than I can possibly say. He was a real artistic guy... sensitive...a painter.

INT. COOK COUNTY JAIL - CAFETERIA - NIGHT

A massive clang of tin plates as a whistle signals the prisoners to sit. CAFETERIA WORKERS move down rows of tables, serving slop from metal pots. We travel past Roxie, who is eavesdropping on a nearby conversation:

MONA
He was always trying to find himself. He'd go out every night looking for himself and on the way he found Ruth, Gladys, Rosemary...and Irving. I guess you could say we broke up because of artistic differences.

INT. "STAGE" - NIGHT

Mona stands over her victim.

MONA
He saw himself as alive, and I saw him dead.

ALL
THE DIRTY BUM, BUM, BUM, BUM, BUM
THE DIRTY BUM, BUM, BUM, BUM, BUM

The set now consists of two tiers of prison cells, teeming with vengeful WOMEN:

LIZ, ANNIE, JUNE, MONA
THEY HAD IT COMING
THEY HAD IT COMING
THEY HAD IT COMING ALL ALONG
'CAUSE IF THEY USED US
AND THEY ABUSED US
HOW COULD YOU TELL US
THAT WE WERE WRONG

VELMA & HUNYAK
THEY HAD IT COMING

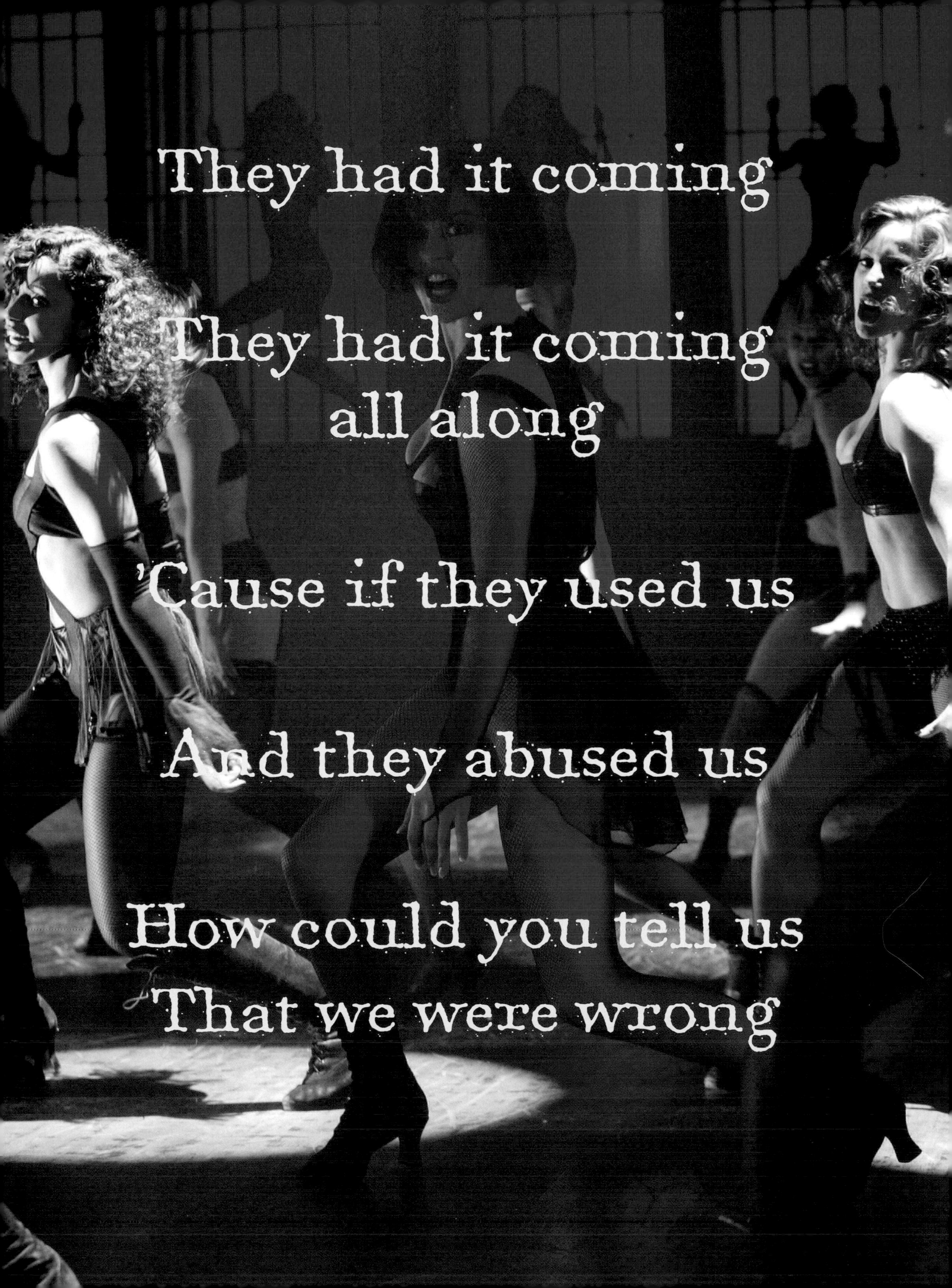

They had it coming

They had it coming
all along

'Cause if they used us

And they abused us

How could you tell us
That we were wrong

THEY HAD IT COMING
THEY HAD IT COMING ALL ALONG
'CAUSE IF THEY USED US
AND THEY ABUSED US
HOW COULD YOU TELL US
THAT WE WERE WRONG

ALL (CONT'D)
HE HAD IT COMING
HE HAD IT COMING
HE ONLY HAD HIMSELF TO BLAME
IF YOU'D HAVE BEEN THERE
IF YOU'D HAVE SEEN IT
I BETCHA YOU WOULD HAVE DONE THE SAME!

Another layer of bars descends in front of the women. Their voices overlap and start to fade:

LIZ
You pop that gum one more time!

ANNIE
Single my ass.

JUNE
Ten times!

HUNYAK
Miert esukott Uncle Same bortonbe.

VELMA
Number Seventeen — the spread eagle.

MONA
Artistic differences.

INT. CELL BLOCK - NIGHT
The rhythm continues. Weeks have passed but Roxie still lies awake, listening to the dripping faucet....a faraway scream...some light snoring.

Roxie curls up and tries to get some sleep.

INT. COOK COUNTY JAIL - LAUNDRY - DAY
Inmates feed laundry into huge, primitive washing machines. Roxie, dripping sweat, loads clean sheets and towels into a bin. Next to her, the Hunyak carefully irons some dainty silk lingerie. Roxie turns to Annie and June.

ROXIE
Who belongs to them?

JUNE
What's it to you?

ROXIE
Nothin'. I heard they were Velma's.

ANNIE
Yeah, the Hunyak does all her laundry for a dollar a week.

Roxie turns, watches the Hunyak folding Velma's lingerie on the ironing board.

INT. COOK COUNTY JAIL - HALLWAY - DAY (LATER)
Roxie stands outside the matron's office. A guard glances up.

ROXIE
Fresh towels for the can.

The guard nods sourly. He unlocks the bathroom door.

GUARD
Make it quick.

INT. COOK COUNTY JAIL - MATRON'S BATHROOM - DAY
Roxie replaces the dirty towels. Through a door that's slightly ajar:

MATRON (O.S.)
...Billy Flynn's set your trial date for March 5th. March 7th you'll be acquitted, and March 8th — do you know what Mama's gonna do for you? She's gonna put you back on the vaudeville circuit.

Roxie adjusts the cupboard mirror to let her see into the office. Velma stands opposite the matron, who reaches up to light her cigarette.

VELMA
So now you're an agent too?

MATRON
Well, dearie...until Ma Bell installs a private line in your cell, all the calls have gotta go through me.

VELMA
What kind of dough are we talking about?

MATRON
It's a crazy world. Babe Ruth is wearing rouge and playing the Palace for five thousand a week.

VELMA
Yeah, and what about someone with real talent?

MATRON
Well, I been talkin' to the boys over at William Morris and due to your recent sensational activities they think they can get you twenty-five hundred.

Roxie and Velma are both flabbergasted.

VELMA
Twenty-five hundred! The most me and Veronica ever made together was three-fifty.

MATRON
That's what happens—you got the right representation.

VELMA
You know, Mama, I always wanted to play Big Jim Colisimo's. Do you think you could get me that?

MATRON
Big Jim's! Jeez, I don't know. That's gonna take another phone call.

VELMA
And how much is that gonna cost me?

MATRON
Come on, Vel, you know how I feel about you. You're like family to me — like my own. I'll do it for fifty bucks.

Resigned, Velma hikes up her kimono and removes some cash from her garter belt. Roxie's eyes are drawn to the distinctive garter, blue with a rhinestone buckle.

VELMA
Fifty bucks for a phone call. You must get a lot of wrong numbers, Mama.

Velma snubs out her cigarette and heads out. Roxie scoops up the dirty towels and steps back into:

INT. COOK COUNTY JAIL - HALLWAY - DAY
Roxie feigns surprise at seeing Velma.

ROXIE
Oh, Miss Kelly...here's your personals.

She reaches into the bin, takes out Velma's lingerie.

ROXIE (CONT'D) (LYING)
Pressed by yours truly.

Velma takes a dollar bill from her garter.

ROXIE (CONT'D)
No, it's my pleasure.

Roxie holds onto the underwear, trying to keep the conversation going.

ROXIE (CONT'D)
Listen, can I ask you somethin'?

VELMA (NOT MEANING IT)
Sure.

ROXIE
Mr. Harrison said what I done is a hanging case and he's prepared to ask for the maximum penalty.

VELMA
Yeah, so?

ROXIE
So I'm scared. I sure would appreciate a little advice, especially from someone I admire as much as you. See, ever since I can remember, I wanted to be on the stage....

VELMA
What's your talent? Washing and drying?

ROXIE
No, I danced in the chorus. Of course, that was before I met my husband Amos....

Velma's already bored to tears.

VELMA
Look, hon, you want some advice? Here it is, direct from me to you.

She grabs the lingerie from Roxie.

VELMA (CONT'D)
Keep your paws off my underwear. 'Kay?

ROXIE
'Kay.

Velma walks off.

ROXIE (CONT'D)
Thanks for nothin'.

MATRON
She's something, ain't she?

Roxie turns, surprised to see the matron.

MATRON (CONT'D)
No matter how big she gets, she's still as common as ever.

She rubs Roxie's shoulder.

MATRON (CONT'D)
I'd like to help you, dearie.

Fashions of the Times

Creating the costumes for *Chicago* was like working on two movies, one set in the real world of everyday life and the other in the surreal world of Roxie's fantasy theater. Costume designer Colleen Atwood began by researching the real world of the '20s, trying to discover "what people on the street looked like, what people wore, how much money most people had."

Using newspapers, newsreels, and photo albums for background, Atwood scoured costume rental agencies in the United States and London for period clothes. "I really wanted to use as much real stuff as I could," she says, "because I knew I was going to make all the stage clothes." The film's extras wore rental costumes, while the clothes worn by *Chicago*'s principals were mostly designed by Atwood.

Still in a couple of instances, Atwood found vintage clothing that worked magic on the stars. For Richard Gere's flashy Billy Flynn she found a medium-gray suit with a belt in back. "It fit perfectly, but it wasn't only the fit—it had the right feeling for the character. Billy Flynn's rich, but he's nouveau riche. He's just a little quirky, like his suit has maybe one too many bells and whistles on it." For Catherine Zeta-Jones' Velma she found a "beautiful rich blue velvet coat," which she wears early on in the film.

"Each actor's character in the story is revealed in different ways," says Atwood. "Velma opens the movie as a very strong character, and her colors are black and bold. She has a complete fearlessness. Roxie's character was the most complex because we see her in a real world, and then we see everyone else through her eyes in the

RIGHT BACKGROUND: Colleen Atwood's "look board" for women's costumes. Right inset: Archival image of women's dress, 1926

fantasies. For her real world I used an almost skin-toned palette. But her fantasy colors were much stronger and more vibrant."

In the glamorous world of Roxie's imaginary theater, everyone looks good, everyone looks sexy (well, except for her cuckolded husband, Amos, who wears a tramp's outfit). From the erotic bondage motif of "Cell Block Tango" to the burlesque of "All I Care About" to the circus atmosphere of "Razzle Dazzle," the costumes leave long, bare limbs waving across the screen like cilia.

In "All I Care About," Atwood says with a laugh, "Rob Marshall wanted the girls to have flash, he wanted them almost naked but not quite. And since the song's about love, we used pinks and reds. The costumes just kept getting smaller, and when the girls first saw the costumes, they were going, 'Oh, my God.' So we put a little fringe on them, customizing each outfit to cover the different needs that people had."

For Marshall, Atwood's skimpy costumes are not just artful; they also reflect something about the times. "Colleen has a great, unique vision, and that's really what I wanted," says Marshall. "She understood the freedom of that era, and the sexuality of that era. She knew how much skin needed to be there."

"It was wilder then than today," Atwood says. "We've all been through different eras of wildness. But they were coming out the Victorian era. So I think it led to the insanity of the period. You weren't supposed to drink, but everyone drank gin. You got rid of the corset, and then suddenly people were running around with these little flimsy dresses on and no underwear. It must have been so exciting for people because they never thought that life could be that way. People like Roxie saw a chance to get ahead with it all and took it."

BACKGROUND: Colleen Atwood's "look board" for men's costumes. RIGHT: Richard Gere as Billy Flynn and barely clad chorines in "All I Care About."

The matron leads Roxie into her office. She winks at the guard and pulls the door shut.

INT. MATRON'S OFFICE - DAY
The matron points to a chair.

> **MATRON**
> Take a load off.

Roxie sits, careful to let her uniform ride up her thigh.

> **MATRON** (CONT'D)
> So what do you figure on using for grounds?

> **ROXIE**
> Grounds?

> **MATRON**
> What are you gonna tell the jury?

> **ROXIE**
> I guess…I'll just tell them the truth.

> **MATRON**
> Telling the truth, that's a one-way ticket to the death house.

> **ROXIE**
> Holy Mother of God…

> **MATRON**
> Relax. In this town, murder's a form of entertainment.

[The matron says that no woman has been hanged in Cook County for 47 years.]

> **ROXIE**
> Oh, Jesus, Mary and Joseph…

> **MATRON**
> You're talking to the wrong people. What you need is Billy Flynn.

> **ROXIE**
> How do you get this…Billy Flynn?

> **MATRON**
> Not by praying, dearie. First you give me a hundred dollars, then I make a phone call.

> **ROXIE**
> A hundred? But you just, I mean…

She catches herself.

> **ROXIE** (CONT'D)
> …that seems pretty steep for a phone call.

The matron stands, moves around the desk.

> **MATRON**
> He's worth every cent.

From Roxie's POV, we see the wall behind the matron become transparent, revealing the dim outline of INMATES standing behind bars.

> **WOMEN**
> WE WANT BILLY…

Roxie tries to stay focused on the matron.

The matron puts her hand on Roxie's knee.

> **ROXIE**
> He never lost a case?

> **MATRON**
> Never.

The women slide up and down the cell bars, as the light continues to cross-fade. The matron is silhouetted now.

> **WOMEN**
> WHERE IS BILLY…

> **MATRON**
> Every girl in this place would kill to have Billy Flynn represent her.

INT. "STAGE" - NIGHT
The inmates' hands reach through the cell bars.

> **INMATES**
> GIVE US BILLY
> WE WANT BILLY

The women undo their buttons.

> **INMATES** (CONT'D)
> B—I—DOUBLE L—Y
> WE'RE ALL HIS

The inmates shed their uniforms, looking practically nude in their slightly worn showgirl costumes.

> **INMATES** (CONT'D)
> HE'S OUR KIND OF A GUY
> AND OOH WHAT LUCK
> 'CAUSE HERE HE IS.

The cell bars ride off, revealing a set of stairs.

> **BANDLEADER**
> Ladies and gentlemen, presenting the Silver Tongued Prince of the Courtroom — the one — the only Billy Flynn.

At the top of the stairs, a DAPPER MAN is getting

We want Billy...

Richard Gere

Richard Gere, who plays the slick and wily attorney Billy Flynn, was honest with director Rob Marshall when they first met about the part. "I said to Rob, 'Look, I can sing this, but I don't know if I could tap dance.' But he said, 'Well, we'll see.' So that was the only issue for me."

In the end, it was a complete nonissue, for Gere is mesmerizing as he tap dances his final arguments during Roxie's murder trial in the song "Razzle Dazzle." Perhaps that's not so surprising since Gere began his acting career in musicals in the early '70s. His first audition, when he was just 21, was for a rock musical called *Soon*, and he played Danny in a West End production of *Grease*. He is also an accomplished pianist and music composer.

Still, he went back to school with assistant choreographer Cynthia Onrubia, who had worked with Marshall on *Cabaret* and *Victor/Victoria*. "Cynthia was just a great teacher," says Gere. "She's one of the great tap dancers on Broadway. She was fabulous. So when we finally shot, we had a lot of fun."

Marshall himself never had any doubts about Gere. "I just trusted him," he says. "I thought, He's the perfect Billy Flynn. I was right. He really is. I lucked out."

But beyond the singing and dancing, what really attracted Gere to *Chicago* was Bill Condon's script. "I thought it was really smart how he had taken this kind of Dennis Potter approach to the material, where a lot of it is in Renée's mind, in Roxie's mind. She's projecting her images of events, and people, like a child does. So it had this kind of child-like innocence, but that's juxtaposed with the hard reality of a murder case in Chicago in the '20s.

"The interesting thing about the songs," he continues, "is that they're all projections from her mind, so when we meet, she sees me as her protector. I'm the one who can get you off. She has this vision of me as a kind of a Lancelot character who just goes around helping women in distress, which is—as you see in the movie— very far from the truth. My song 'All I Care About' is based on that vision."

Gere also appreciated the film's satire of the judicial system. "The piece is about the symbiotic nature of everyone involved with this judiciary show business, the whole judicial court system," he says. "It's very cynical about it, and for good reason. We live in an age where that's in our face all the time."

his shoes shined in silhouette. He stands and flips a dime to the SHOE-SHINE MAN, who tips his hat to catch the coin. The shoe-shine man turns — it's BILLY FLYNN. He glides down the steps.

> **BILLY**
> I DON'T CARE ABOUT EXPENSIVE THINGS
> CASHMERE COATS, DIAMOND RINGS
> DON'T MEAN A THING
> ALL I CARE ABOUT IS LOVE

> **BILLY** (CONT'D)
> THAT'S WHAT I'M HERE FOR

> **GIRLS**
> THAT'S WHAT HE'S HERE FOR

The girls strike broken poses. More Minsky's than Ziegfeld.

INT. BILLY'S OFFICE - DAY
Billy dictates notes to an ASSISTANT as he is fussed over by tailors. Fabrics fit for a millionaire, but cut in a flashy way to impress the common man.

> **BILLY** (V.O.)
> I DON'T CARE FOR WEARING SILK CRAVATS
> RUBY STUDS, SATIN SPATS
> DON'T MEAN A THING

Billy checks the cut in a mirror. Frustrated, he kicks a TAILOR trying to hem his pant leg.

INT. "STAGE" - NIGHT
Billy kicks his way across the stage.

> **BILLY**
> ALL I CARE ABOUT IS LOVE

> **GIRLS**
> ALL HE CARES ABOUT IS LOVE

> **BILLY**
> GIMME TWO EYES OF BLUE
> SOFTLY SAYING, "I NEED YOU"
> LET ME SEE HER STANDIN' THERE
> AND HONEST MISTER, I'M A MILLIONAIRE

EXT. STATE STREET - DAY (LATER)
Billy breezes over to his Rolls-Royce. His CHAUF-FEUR opens the door for him.

INT. "STAGE" - NIGHT
The chorus resembles the shape of the Rolls-Royce, with the front dancer playing the Winged Victory hood ornament.

> **BILLY**
> I DON'T CARE FOR ANY FINE ATTIRE
> VANDERBILT MIGHT ADMIRE
> NO, NO, NOT ME

Billy cranks a dancer's leg, pretending to set the parking brake.

> **BILLY** (CONT'D)
> ALL I CARE ABOUT IS LOVE

Two other girls create a door, which Billy steps through.

> **GIRLS**
> ALL HE CARES ABOUT IS LOVE

EXT. COOK COUNTY JAIL - DAY
Billy whistles as he heads up the prison steps.

INT. COOK COUNTY JAIL - HALLWAY - DAY
Inmates reach through the bars of the cell block open area, as Billy sweeps past, still whistling.

> **BILLY**
> Good morning, ladies.

> **HUNYAK**
> Not guilty! Not guilty!

> **BILLY**
> You tell 'em, sweetheart.

INT. "STAGE" - NIGHT
The girls swing Billy in their arms.

> **GIRLS**
> THAT'S WHAT HE'S HERE FOR

INT. COOK COUNTY JAIL - COMMON ROOM - DAY (LATER)
A small press conference, half a dozen reporters and a few PHOTOGRAPHERS. MARY SUNSHINE, a sob sister for the *Evening Star*, nods sympathetically as Velma tells her story.

> **MARY SUNSHINE**
> Miss Kelly, do you remember anything at all about that night?

[Velma says that the only thing she remembers is that she didn't do it.]

> **MARY SUNSHINE**
> Any idea who did, dear?

> **BILLY**
> No, but my client is offering a substantial reward to anyone with information about this crime.

Gimme two eyes of blue
Softly saying,
"I need you"
Let me see her standin' there
And honest mister, I'm a millionaire

This is obviously news to Velma.

MARY SUNSHINE
How much is the reward, Miss Kelly?

VELMA (TO BILLY)
I don't know. How much?

BILLY
We'll work that out after the trial.
(stands)
Now, if there are no more questions,
Miss Kelly and I have a lot of work to do.

Billy leads Velma off.

VELMA
What's all this about a reward?

BILLY
[The reporters will] write it up wrong and
later on you can deny the whole thing.

INT. "STAGE" - NIGHT
Moving through the dancers' legs:

GIRLS
ALL HE CARES ABOUT IS LOVE!

INT. COOK COUNTY JAIL - SECURITY AREA - DAY
Velma is escorted up a spiral staircase by a GUARD,
while Billy waits for another GUARD to let him out
of the secure area.

ROXIE (THROUGH BARS)
Oh, Mr. Flynn! Mr. Flynn!

Billy steps out of the secure area, waits for the
guard to unlock the outer gate.

ROXIE (CONT'D)
I'm Roxie Hart.

BILLY
Who?

ROXIE
Mama talked to you about me.

BILLY
Oh, yeah, right. The cute one.

He checks her out, likes what he sees. The second
gate opens.

ROXIE
I was hoping you might represent me.

BILLY
You got five thousand dollars?

ROXIE
Gee, that's a lot of money. Mama didn't say anything about five thousand dollars.

Billy steps into the outer hallway and keeps going. Roxie scrambles to keep up.

ROXIE (CONT'D)
Lookit, Mr. Flynn, I've never been very good at this sort of thing. But couldn't we make some kind of arrangement between us? I can be an awfully good sport.

She smiles knowingly. Billy laughs.

BILLY (OVER HIS SHOULDER)
Call me when you got five thousand dollars.

He leaves, whistling again.

INT. "STAGE" - NIGHT
The girls roll on their backs, creating a human wave for Billy to ride. He grabs a dancer's boa as she circles him.

BILLY
SHOW ME LONG, LONG RAVEN HAIR

FLOWIN' DOWN, ABOUT TO THERE
WHEN I SEE HER RUNNIN' FREE
KEEP YOUR MONEY, THAT'S ENOUGH FOR ME

Billy digs into a girl's cleavage, comes up with a handful of coins. He tosses them out as silver coins rain down on the stage. Billy moves down the runway, stripping off his vest and suspenders.

BILLY (CONT'D)
I DON'T CARE FOR DRIVIN' PACKARD CARS
OR SMOKING LONG, BUCK CIGARS
NO, NO, NOT ME

He rips off his pants.

GIRLS
WHOA!

BILLY
ALL I CARE ABOUT IS

Billy backs up, pulling off his shirt.

BILLY (CONT'D)
DOIN' THE GUY IN
WHO'S PICKIN' ON YOU
TWISTIN' THE WRIST
THAT'S TURNIN' THE SCREW

Billy stands on the stairs, wearing only his hat, t-shirt, boxers, and a cigar. A curtain opens, revealing six girls in a candelabra tableau.

> **BILLY** (CONT'D)
> ALL I CARE ABOUT IS LOVE!

> **ALL**
> ALL HE CARES ABOUT IS LOVE!

The girls in front provide cover as Billy pulls off his boxers and swings them above his head. The number ends.

INT. BILLY'S LAW FIRM - OUTER OFFICE - DAY

Amos is perched uncomfortably on a small chair. It's clear he's been waiting a while. Billy's SECRE-TARY finally appears.

> **BILLY'S SECRETARY**
> Oh. He'll see you now.

INT. BILLY'S OFFICE - DAY

Billy's ASSISTANT leaves as Amos enters. Billy looks up, offers Amos a blank smile.

> **BILLY**
> Well, hello, Andy.

> **AMOS**
> Amos. My name is Amos.

> **BILLY**
> That's right. Have a seat.

Amos does as he is told.

> **BILLY** (CONT'D)
> You know, you're a remarkable man.

> **AMOS**
> Huh?

> **BILLY**
> Your wife two-times you, plugs the guy, and then tries to pin it on you. Most men'd let a dame like that swing. But you're sticking by her and that makes you a hero in my eyes.

Amos frowns, confused.

> **AMOS**
> Right. I'm a hero.

> **BILLY**
> Did you bring the money?

> **AMOS**
> I didn't do as well as I hoped.

> (puts up a restraining hand)
> But I will, Mr. Flynn. I will.

He takes certificates and savings bonds from his pockets. Billy flips through them.

[It's clear that Amos doesn't have enough money. He offers to pay Billy out of his paycheck each week.]

> **BILLY**
> You don't have five thousand dollars so I figure you're a dirty liar, and I don't waste my time with dirty liars.

Billy swings around in his chair, his back to Amos now. The meeting is over.

> **AMOS**
> Look, I'm real sorry, Mr. Flynn.

Amos starts to gather the cash and certificates. Billy swings back around.

> **BILLY**
> On the other hand, your devotion to your wife is really very touching.

Billy puts his hand on the money and slides it into his desk drawer.

> **BILLY** (CONT'D)
> Now look, Hart, I don't like to blow my own horn, but believe me, if Jesus Christ had lived in Chicago today — and if he had five thousand dollars and had come to me — things would have turned out differently.

Billy moves over to the window, the city spread out beneath him. [He describes his fundraising scheme—an auction.]

> **BILLY** (CONT'D)
> Here's what we're gonna do. By the end of the week I'll have Roxie's name on the front page of every newspaper in town. Sweetest little jazz killer ever to hit Chicago — that's the angle I'm after. Then we announce we're gonna hold an auction. Tell 'em we got to raise money for her defense. They'll buy anything she ever touched...

INT. COOK COUNTY JAIL - HOLDING ROOM - DAY

Billy lays out his plan for Roxie, who looks excited.

> **BILLY**
> ...your shoes, your dresses, your perfume, your underwear...

ROXIE
And Victrola records. Like the one I was playing when I shot that bastard.

BILLY
I never heard that.

ROXIE
Not that I didn't have grounds.
(a beat)
Any idea what they were?

BILLY
That's for when we go to trial. Nobody's going to care a lick what your defense is unless they care about you.

Roxie nods, genuinely impressed.

BILLY (CONT'D)
The first thing we got to do is work up some sympathy from the press. They're not all pushovers like Mary Sunshine. But there's one thing they can never resist and that's a reformed sinner. So tell me, what was your favorite subject in school?

ROXIE
Oh I was a real dummy.

BILLY
You must have been good at something.

ROXIE
I got high marks for courtesy and helpfulness.

BILLY
Perfect. You wanted to be a nun.

ROXIE
A nun!

[After Roxie describes her humble upbringing, Billy spins her story: She was born into a refined Southern home, but lost her fortune at a young age. Raised by nuns, she was caught up in a runaway marriage. Out of loneliness and despair, she succumbed to the temptations of jazz and liquor.]

BILLY
You have sinned and you are sorry.

ROXIE
That's beautiful.

MONTAGE

A short musical interlude, as Roxie prepares for her debut:

INT. COOK COUNTY JAIL - ROXIE'S CELL - NIGHT
Roxie polishes a spoon, then uses it to gaze at her reflection. She compares her eyes with Mary Pickford's, whose picture is taped on the wall.

BILLY (V.O.)
Kid — when I'm through with you, not only will you be acquitted — every man on that jury'll want to take you home to meet his mother.

Roxie plucks her eyebrows to resemble America's sweetheart.

INT. COOK COUNTY JAIL - MATRON'S OFFICE - DAY
Roxie rehearses her story for Billy and the matron:

ROXIE
I was born on a beautiful Southern convent.

MATRON
What?

Billy shakes his head in despair.

ROXIE
Holy shit! I'll never get this straight.

BILLY
Pipe down on the swearing. From here on in, you say nothing rougher than "Oh, dear." Now try again.

INT. COOK COUNTY JAIL - ROXIE'S CELL - NIGHT
Roxie sketches a few different hair designs in her silver diary.

INT. COOK COUNTY JAIL - CELL BLOCK - DAY
The inmates line up for morning inspection. Roxie slips a fiver to the matron, who passes her a small tube of hair dye.

INT. COOK COUNTY JAIL - BATHROOM - NIGHT
Roxie dyes her roots in the empty bathroom.

INT. COOK COUNTY JAIL - ROXIE'S CELL - NIGHT
In the middle of the night, Roxie sits on her cot, cutting her hair to resemble Mary Pickford's.

INT. COOK COUNTY JAIL - COMMON ROOM - DAY
Velma sits opposite Billy Flynn.

VELMA
I came up with some more things to do on the witness stand. I thought I could get all

teary-eyed and ask to borrow your handkerchief. Then I'll take a peek at the jury and flash 'em a bit of thigh, like this.

She opens her legs, revealing the distinctive rhinestone garter.

BILLY (LOOKING PAST HER)
Sounds great.

Velma turns, sees Roxie and the matron at the top of the stairs. Roxie makes a grand entrance, her hair fashioned in a blonde bob, with a signature triple curl across one side. It's innocent but also a little sassy. Billy stands.

VELMA
Hey...don't you want to hear the rest?

BILLY
Tomorrow, kiddo. You're at the top of my list.

He moves over to Roxie.

BILLY (CONT'D)
Well, well...

She affects a sweet smile.

ROXIE
I'm so sorry to be late, Mr. Flynn.
(eyes Velma)
Hope you weren't too bored.

Billy chuckles, pulls out a chair for her. Velma fumes quietly in the corner.

INT. COOK COUNTY JAIL - HALLWAY (LATER) - NIGHT
Roxie reads the Bible, her mouth moving while she reads.

VELMA (O.S.)
Hey, Pollyanna.

Roxie looks up. Velma's just come from the showers.

VELMA (CONT'D)
I heard your press conference is tomorrow.

ROXIE
What's it to you?

VELMA
You wanted my advice? Here it is. You might be payin' the bills, but don't forget — Billy Flynn's number one client is Billy Flynn.

ROXIE
Meaning what?

Roxie is interested in spite of herself.

VELMA
Don't let him hog the spotlight. Remember, you're the one they paid to see.

Velma moves off.

INT. COURTHOUSE - CORRIDOR - DAY (CONTINUOUS)
Billy leads Roxie toward the exit.

BILLY
Now remember, we can only sell them one idea at a time....

ROXIE
I can still see him comin' at me with that awful look in his eyes.

BILLY
And?

ROXIE
We both reached for the gun.

BILLY
That's right. You both reached for the gun.

They arrive at the door.

BILLY (CONT'D)
Ready?

Roxie takes a deep breath, nods. Billy opens the door.

EXT. COOK COUNTY COURTHOUSE STEPS - DAY
Roxie and Billy walk to a bank of radio microphones. Dozens of REPORTERS, flashbulbs, newsreel cameras, all in Roxie's face.

PHOTOGRAPHERS (IN UNISON)
This way, Roxie! Give us a smile, Roxie! Over here, Rox!

BILLY
Good day, gentlemen, Miss Sunshine.
My client has just entered a plea of not guilty, and we look forward to a trial at the earliest possible date. Now, if there are any questions...

He points to Mary Sunshine.

MARY SUNSHINE
As you know, my paper is dry. Do you have any advice for young girls seeking to avoid a life of jazz and drink?

Roxie leans forward, but Billy answers for her:

Christine Baranski

In the original musical Christine Baranski's character Mary Sunshine was the vaudeville act of a drag queen. That just wouldn't do in the film version. "In our production we have reality," explains director Rob Marshall. "We don't just have vaudeville. We couldn't have a man playing a woman in reality. So Mary Sunshine became a woman, and Christine Baranski and I had to invent our way through it, because it wasn't on the page.

"So Bill Condon, Christine, and I created this savvy news lady—the Liz Smith of her time—who was a sob sister. And we worked on getting a sense that she was as complicit and corrupt as everyone else."

Baranski also sees her character in contemporary terms. "Mary in this version is like a Barbara Walters or a Diane Sawyer," Baranski says, "somebody who specializes in sincerity, who's very nice, you know, but who gets the story because these women open up to her when she interviews them. They open up, and then she spins it a certain way as this-poor-creature-is-a-victim."

And the journalist Mary has a "symbiotic" relationship with the defense lawyer. "Billy Flynn knows that Mary's the one who will spin it a certain way because it's all about getting public sympathy and having these murderesses be perceived as victims," Baranski says. "It's like 'I use you, you use me.' The journalists are manipulated but then they also know they can sell newspapers if they spin it a certain way."

BILLY
Absolutely. Mrs. Hart feels that it was it was the tragic combination of liquor and jazz which led to her downfall.

He points to another reporter, but Roxie leans into the microphones.

ROXIE
Ladies and gentlemen, I'm just so flattered y'all came to see me.

She affects a sweet tragic look, and speaks in the worst refined Southern accent you've ever heard.

ROXIE (CONT'D)
See, I was a moth...a moth crushed on the wheel.

Confusion spreads among the reporters as Roxie mangles her metaphors.

ROXIE (CONT'D)
You know, a butterfly...drawn to the flame.

Realizing she's screwed up, she offers a lovely, wistful smile.

ROXIE (CONT'D)
I guess you want to know why I shot the bastard.

Billy grabs Roxie by the back of her hair.

BILLY
Shut up, dummy.

INT. "STAGE" - DAY
Billy sits on a wooden chair, with a ventriloquist's DUMMY on his lap. It's a two-foot high version of Roxie, with the same bob and the same dress.

BANDLEADER
Mr. Billy Flynn in the "Press Conference Rag." Notice how his mouth never moves — almost.

Behind them, "marionette" REPORTERS sit lifelessly. In the club, there's a casual matinee crowd.

EXT. COOK COUNTY COURTHOUSE - DAY
Billy points to a REPORTER.

REPORTER
Where'd you come from?

INT. "STAGE" - DAY
The dummy opens its eyes.

BILLY/ROXIE DUMMY
MISSISSIPPI.

EXT. COOK COUNTY COURTHOUSE - DAY

Another REPORTER calls out a question:

> **REPORTER #2**
> And your parents?

INT. "STAGE" - DAY

The dummy flutters its eyelashes coyly.

> **BILLY/ROXIE DUMMY**
> VERY WEALTHY.

EXT. COOK COUNTY COURTHOUSE - DAY

A third REPORTER:

> **REPORTER #3**
> Where are they now?

INT. "STAGE" - DAY

The dummy makes a sign of the cross.

> **BILLY/ROXIE DUMMY**
> SIX FEET UNDER.

EXT. COOK COUNTY COURTHOUSE - DAY

Roxie's about to answer when Billy jumps in.

> **BILLY**
> But she was granted one more start...

INT. "STAGE" - DAY

The dummy lowers its head piously.

> **BILLY/ROXIE DUMMY**
> THE CONVENT OF THE SACRED HEART

EXT. COOK COUNTY COURTHOUSE - DAY

Reporters in back struggle to be noticed:

> **REPORTERS** (IN UNISON)
> Mr. Flynn! This way, Roxie! Over here, Billy!

INT. "STAGE" - DAY

When the dummy lifts its head, we see that it's now Roxie sitting on Billy's lap. Behind them, the reporters stir to life.

> **REPORTER #1**
> WHEN'D YOU GET HERE?

> **BILLY/ROXIE**
> 1920.

> **REPORTER #2**
> HOW OLD WERE YOU?

EXT. COOK COUNTY COURTHOUSE - DAY

Roxie shoots Billy a warning look.

INT. "STAGE" - DAY

Roxie shrugs in confusion.

> **BILLY/ROXIE**
> DON'T REMEMBER.

> **REPORTER #3**
> THEN WHAT HAPPENED?

> **BILLY/ROXIE**
> I MET AMOS
> AND HE STOLE MY HEART AWAY
> CONVINCED ME TO ELOPE ONE DAY

EXT. COOK COUNTY COURTHOUSE - DAY

Mary Sunshine scribbles furiously.

> **MARY SUNSHINE**
> You poor dear! I can't believe what you've been
> through! A convent girl! A runaway marriage!
> Oh, it's too, too terrible. Now tell us, Roxie:

INT. "STAGE" - DAY

The marionette MARY SUNSHINE lifts her head.

> **MARY SUNSHINE**
> WHO'S FRED CASELY?

Roxie looks down in shame.

> **BILLY/ROXIE**
> MY EX-BOYFRIEND.

> **REPORTERS**
> WHY'D YOU SHOOT HIM?

> **BILLY/ROXIE**
> I WAS LEAVIN'.

> **REPORTERS**
> WAS HE ANGRY?

> **BILLY/ROXIE**
> LIKE A MADMAN!
> STILL I SAID, "FRED, MOVE ALONG"

EXT. COOK COUNTY COURTHOUSE - DAY

Billy pats Roxie's hand paternally.

> **BILLY**
> She knew that she was doing wrong.

INT. "STAGE" - DAY

> **REPORTERS**
> THEN DESCRIBE IT

> **BILLY/ROXIE**
> HE CAME TOWARD ME.

REPORTERS
WITH THE PISTOL?

BILLY/ROXIE
FROM MY BUREAU

REPORTERS
DID YOU FIGHT HIM?

BILLY/ROXIE
LIKE A TIGER

EXT. COOK COUNTY COURTHOUSE - DAY
Billy leans in to explain:

BILLY
He had strength and she had none.

INT. "STAGE" - DAY
Billy holds up Roxie.

BILLY/ROXIE
AND YET WE BOTH REACHED FOR THE GUN
OH YES, OH YES, OH YES WE BOTH
OH YES WE BOTH
OH YES, WE BOTH REACHED FOR
THE GUN, THE GUN, THE GUN, THE GUN
OH YES, WE BOTH REACHED FOR THE GUN,
FOR THE GUN

Roxie continues to nod her head frantically.

EXT. COOK COUNTY COURTHOUSE - DAY
Billy reenacts the struggle for the gun, while Roxie
nods in agreement.

BILLY & REPORTERS (V.O.)
OH YES, OH YES, OH YES THEY BOTH
OH YES THEY BOTH
OH YES, THEY BOTH REACHED FOR
THE GUN, THE GUN, THE GUN, THE GUN
OH YES, THEY BOTH REACHED FOR THE GUN,
FOR THE GUN

INT. "STAGE" - DAY
Billy dances a waltz with Roxie. He controls her movements through a wooden lever attached to her back.

BILLY
UNDERSTANDABLE
UNDERSTANDABLE
YES, IT'S PERFECTLY UNDERSTANDABLE
COMPREHENSIBLE
COMPREHENSIBLE
NOT A BIT REPREHENSIBLE
IT'S SO DEFENSIBLE!

both
ched
the gun

They sit again.

    REPORTERS
    HOW'RE YOU FEELING?

    BILLY/ROXIE
    VERY FRIGHTENED

    MARY SUNSHINE
    ARE YOU SORRY?

EXT. COOK COUNTY COURTHOUSE - DAY
Roxie turns toward the radio microphones.

    ROXIE
    Are you kidding?

Billy grabs her arm and twists it.

INT. "STAGE" - DAY
It's still Billy's voice coming out of Roxie's mouth.

    REPORTERS
    WHAT'S YOUR STATEMENT?

    BILLY/ROXIE
    ALL I'D SAY IS
    THOUGH MY CHOO-CHOO
    JUMPED THE TRACK
    I'D GIVE MY LIFE TO BRING
    HIM BACK

EXT. COOK COUNTY COURTHOUSE/ INT. "STAGE" - DAY
Now the intercutting between reality and fantasy
becomes more frenetic:

    REPORTERS
    AND?

    BILLY/ROXIE
    STAY AWAY FROM

    REPORTERS
    WHAT?

    BILLY/ROXIE
    JAZZ AND LIQUOR.

    REPORTERS
    AND?

    BILLY/ROXIE
    AND THE MEN WHO

    REPORTERS
    WHAT?

    BILLY/ROXIE
    PLAY FOR FUN.

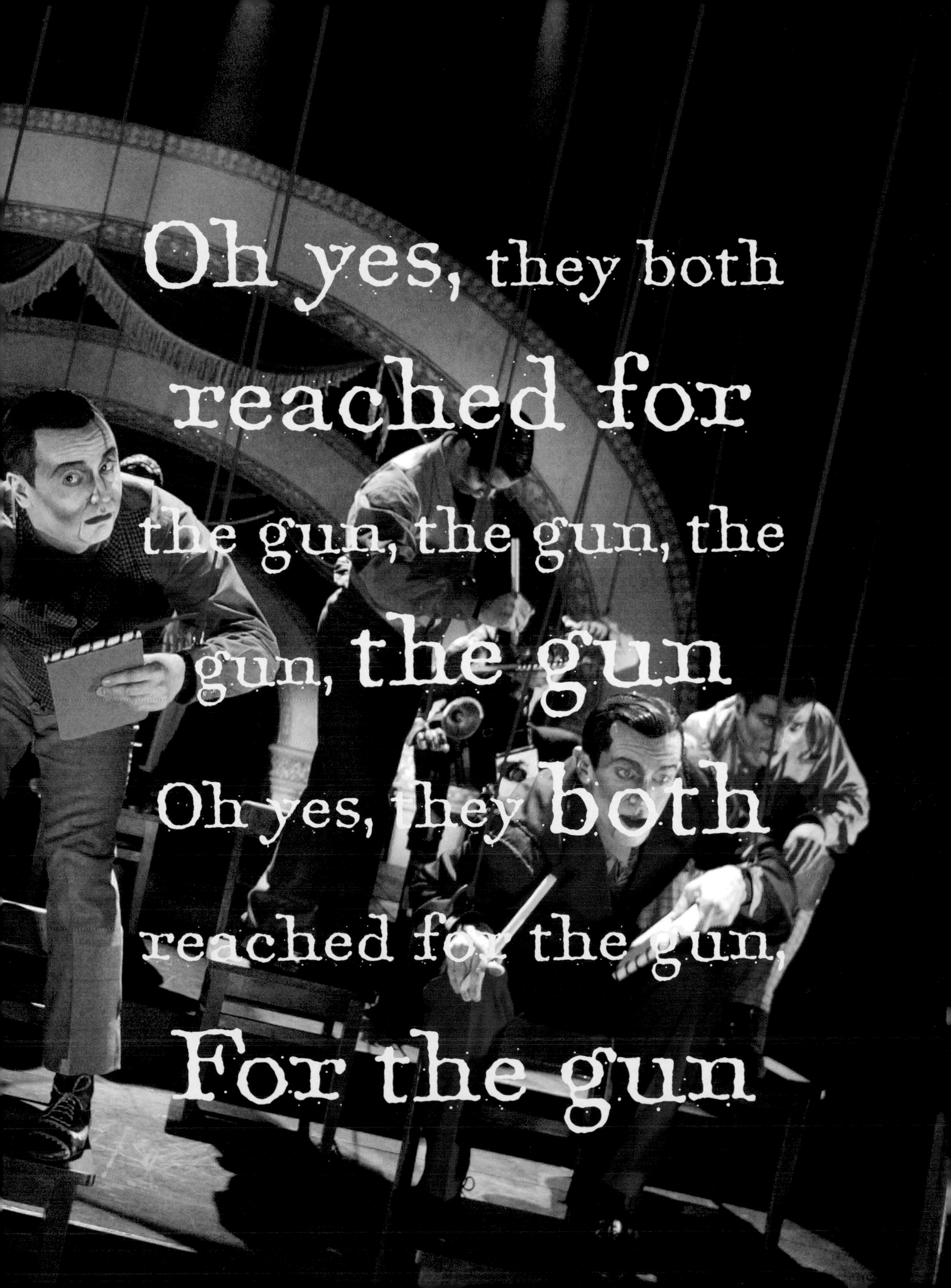
Oh yes, they both
reached for
the gun, the gun, the
gun, the gun
Oh yes, they both
reached for the gun,
For the gun

REPORTERS
AND WHAT?

BILLY/ROXIE
THAT'S THE THOUGHT THAT

REPORTERS
YEAH

BILLY/ROXIE
CAME UPON ME

REPORTERS
WHEN?

Billy turns to the reporters and yells, dropping Roxie on the floor.

BILLY/ROXIE
WHEN WE BOTH REACHED FOR THE GUN

INT. "STAGE" - DAY
Mary Sunshine dances with Billy.

MARY SUNSHINE
UNDERSTANDABLE
UNDERSTANDABLE

BILLY & MARY SUNSHINE
YES, IT'S PERFECTLY UNDERSTANDABLE

Mary Sunshine bounces in mid-air, pulled by strings.

BILLY & MARY SUNSHINE (CONT'D)
COMPREHENSIBLE
COMPREHENSIBLE

Mary Sunshine picks up Roxie and puts her back in Billy's lap.

BILLY & MARY SUNSHINE (CONT'D)
NOT A BIT REPREHENSIBLE
IT'S SO DEFENSIBLE!

REPORTERS
OH YES, OH YES, OH YES THEY BOTH
OH YES THEY BOTH
OH YES, THEY BOTH REACHED FOR

BILLY
Let me hear it.

Billy stands over a marionette box, pulling the strings.

REPORTERS
THE GUN, THE GUN, THE GUN, THE GUN
OH YES, THEY BOTH REACHED FOR THE GUN,
FOR THE GUN

BILLY
Now you got it!

ILLUSTRATED

2 CENTS
CITY and SUBURBS

CHICAGO OBSERVER

LATE NEWS
PICTURES

Vol. 1. No. 1

The Picture Newspaper

48 Pages

BOTH REACHED FOR GUN

(Story on Page 2)

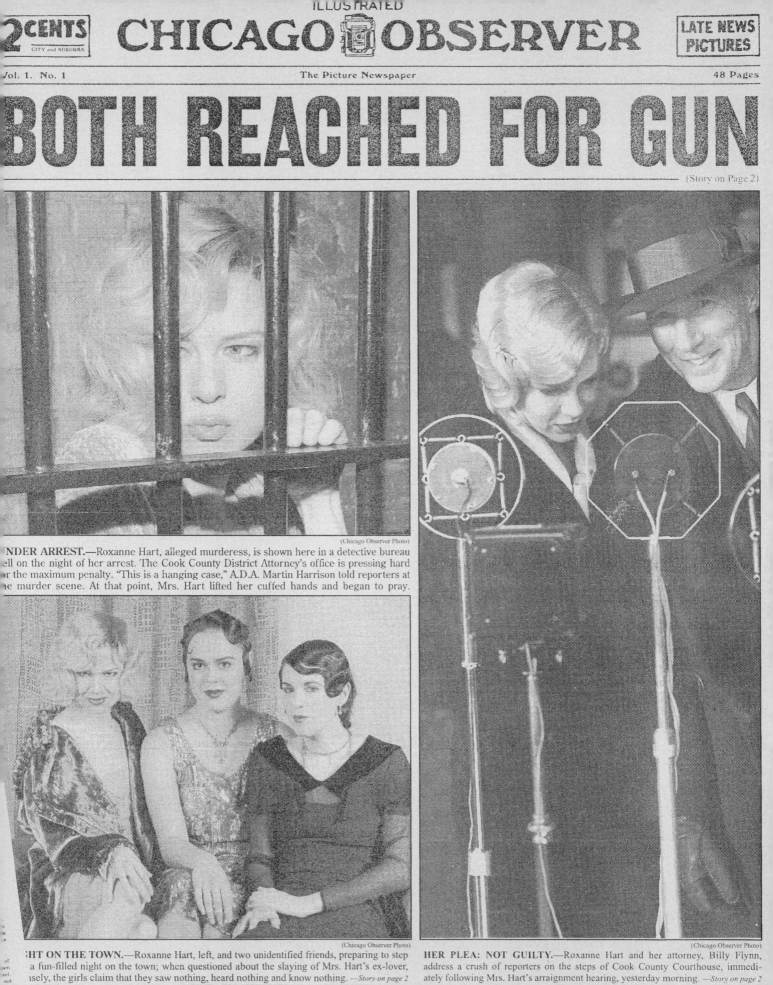

(Chicago Observer Photo)

UNDER ARREST.—Roxanne Hart, alleged murderess, is shown here in a detective bureau cell on the night of her arrest. The Cook County District Attorney's office is pressing hard for the maximum penalty. "This is a hanging case," A.D.A. Martin Harrison told reporters at the murder scene. At that point, Mrs. Hart lifted her cuffed hands and began to pray.

(Chicago Observer Photo)

NIGHT ON THE TOWN.—Roxanne Hart, left, and two unidentified friends, preparing to step out for a fun-filled night on the town; when questioned about the slaying of Mrs. Hart's ex-lover, tersely, the girls claim that they saw nothing, heard nothing and know nothing. —*Story on page 2*

(Chicago Observer Photo)

HER PLEA: NOT GUILTY.—Roxanne Hart and her attorney, Billy Flynn, address a crush of reporters on the steps of Cook County Courthouse, immediately following Mrs. Hart's arraignment hearing, yesterday morning. —*Story on page 2*

$5000 in Prizes for Movie Star Twins

Page
14

INT. "EVENING STAR" NEWSROOM - DAY

Mary Sunshine taps out an article on an Underwood. She rips out the page and hands it to a COPY BOY, who races with it through the chaotic newsroom.

> **REPORTERS** (V.O.)
> OH YES, OH YES, OH YES THEY BOTH
> OH YES THEY BOTH
> OH YES, THEY BOTH REACHED FOR

INT. "STAGE" - DAY

The reporters bob up and down, on marionette strings made of bungee cords.

> **REPORTERS**
> THE GUN, THE GUN, THE GUN, THE GUN
> OH YES, THEY BOTH REACHED FOR THE GUN,
> FOR THE GUN

INT. NEWSROOM - DAY

Hundreds of copies of the *Evening Star* roll off the printing presses.

> **BILLY & REPORTERS** (V.O.)
> OH YES, OH YES, OH YES THEY BOTH
> OH YES THEY BOTH

INT. "STAGE" - DAY

The reporters' movements become more frenetic.

BILLY & REPORTERS
OH YES, THEY BOTH REACHED FOR
THE GUN, THE GUN, THE GUN, THE GUN

EXT. MICHIGAN AVENUE - DAY

Piles of the *Evening Star* are dropped from a delivery truck.

> **BILLY & REPORTERS** (V.O.)
> THE GUN, THE GUN, THE GUN, THE GUN

INT. "STAGE" - DAY

Roxie bounces on Billy's knee.

> **BILLY & REPORTERS**
> THE GUN, THE GUN, THE GUN, THE GUN

EXT. MICHIGAN AVENUE - DAY

At a newsstand, customers grab for one of at least a dozen papers, everything from the morning broadsheets to the early evening tabloids. All run variations on the same headline: THEY BOTH REACHED FOR THE GUN.

> **BILLY & REPORTERS** (V.O.)
> THE GUN, THE GUN, THE GUN, THE GUN

INT. "STAGE" - DAY

Mary Sunshine gives Billy a trick glass of milk.

> **BILLY**
> BOTH REACHED FOR THE GUN

Billy drinks as he holds the last note.

> **REPORTERS**
> THE GUN, THE GUN, THE GUN, THE GUN
> THE GUN, THE GUN, THE GUN, THE GUN

INT. TRAIN STATION - DAY

Moving down a platform full of COMMUTERS reading the morning papers. A sea of headlines, all about Roxie.

> **REPORTERS** (V.O.)
> THE GUN, THE GUN, THE GUN, THE GUN

INT. STAGE - DAY

Everyone dances as the number ends.

> **BILLY & REPORTERS**
> THE GUN, THE GUN, THE GUN, THE GUN
> BOTH REACHED FOR THE GUN
> NEWSREEL FILM

INT. COOK COUNTY JAIL - ROXIE'S CELL - DAY (B&W)

A title spins across the screen: ROXIE ROCKS CHICAGO.

> **NEWSREEL ANNOUNCER** (V.O.)
> Move over, Al Capone. The Windy City has taken a new criminal to its heart. The name on everybody's lips is Roxie Hart, the sweetest little lady ever accused of murder in Chicago.

EXT. BEAUTY PARLOR - DAY (B&W)

Women line up outside a beauty parlor. A sign in the window advertises the now famous triple-curl Roxie bob.

> **NEWSREEL ANNOUNCER** (V.O.)
> Women want to look like her...

A woman exits the shop, shows off her new look to her boyfriend.

> **NEWSREEL ANNOUNCER** (V.O.) (CONT'D)
> Fellas want to go out with her...some little girls even want to take her home...

A toy store window is filled with Roxie dolls. Outside, a little girl smiles, holds up her doll.

> **NEWSREEL ANNOUNCER** (CONT'D)
> Don't get any ideas, little lady. On the other side of town...

INT. COURTHOUSE - HALLWAY - DAY (B&W)

Assistant D.A. Harrison stands stiffly in front of a bank of radio microphones.

> **NEWSREEL ANNOUNCER** (V.O.)
> The Assistant D.A. promises that the game little sharpshooter will swing before the year is out.

Harrison basks in the press attention.

> **NEWSREEL ANNOUNCER** (V.O.) (CONT'D)
> Who knows? If he lives up to his word, Assistant D.A. Harrison might become Governor Harrison someday. Back at the scene of the crime...

INT. ROXIE'S APARTMENT - DAY (B&W)

Curiosity seekers attend the auction at Roxie's South Side apartment. A sailor in line already has Roxie's name tattooed on his forearm.

Choreography

The dance numbers in *Chicago* began, not with hoofers in a studio, but with people sitting around a table talking. Director-choreographer Rob Marshall and his collaborators—associate choreographers Joey Pizzi and Cynthia Onrubia, assistant choreographer Denise Faye, and choreographic supervisor John DeLuca—generally devoted an entire week to conceptualizing the choreography for each song.

Marshall saw Bob Fosse's original Broadway version twice as a teenager and remembers it with almost dreamlike clarity. But while Marshall acknowledges Fosse's influence, he put his own stamp on the film's choreography.

"I'm not Bob Fosse," says Marshall emphatically. "I love Bob Fosse. So I would never want to bastardize his work. I don't want to do watered-down Bob Fosse. His spirit will always be part of it. But over my career, I've had to follow Fosse and Michael Bennett, and I've learned that when you're revising a work, you have to reconceptualize it. And that's just what we did with *Chicago*. It's what I did for *Cabaret*. Our version was more stripped-down and seedier than the original musical or the film."

How does that creative process work? Marshall cites the song "We Both Reached for the Gun." "In the musical, Billy Flynn does a ventriloquist act with Roxie on his lap, feeding her her lines at a press conference. We took that further, seeing Billy as a puppet master and all of the reporters as marionettes.

"In 'Cell Block Tango,' as another example, Fosse used portable cell bars, lit from the bottom, and the revival used chairs. But I thought the tango is something you do with a partner, and then I saw the dancers partnering with their victims."

Extensive research also contributed to the choreography. "Each number had its own character and personality," says associate choreographer Pizzi. "We researched the period to incorporate dances of the 1920s. Also some numbers were inspired by vaudeville performers and movies. You see the Charleston in 'Reach for the Gun,' the Ziegfeld Follies in 'All He Cares About,' Sophie Tucker in Queen Latifah's 'When You're Good to Mama,' and *Showboat* in Renée Zellweger's 'Funny Honey.'"

Only after crafting the big concept for each song did the choreographers get up on their feet. Marshall and his staff spent the summer of 2001 working with dancers on fine-tuning the numbers.

Then the stars went into training, and they drilled for six weeks in Toronto in what was basically dance boot camp. "We'd go from dance rehearsals to voice rehearsals to acting rehearsals," Queen Latifah recalls. "It was a lot of work, initially, but it was great. It made it a lot smoother."

"It took that long," says Renée Zellweger, "because Rob has an extraordinary work ethic, and it was important to him to get it right. And, uh, clearly there was work to be done, especially on my part."

Marshall, in full drill sergeant mode, sums up the experience: "We worked really hard in the rehearsal process. But they wanted to be worked hard. All of them."

ABOVE: Rob Marshall. RIGHT: Renée Zellweger and the other dancers are put through the paces during rehearsal.

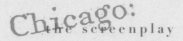

NEWSREEL NARRATOR (V.O.)
Everybody wants a little piece of Roxie Hart.

In the apartment, a man forks over money to
Amos, while his excited wife holds up a used jar of
cold cream.

NEWSREEL NARRATOR (V.O.) (CONT'D)
This jar of cold cream set her husband back
twenty dollars.

Another woman sprays herself with the dregs of
Roxie's perfume.

NEWSREEL NARRATOR (V.O.) (CONT'D)
Maybe this pretty little lady will get some of
that famous Roxie style.

The woman turns to her husband and pretends to
shoot him. They both laugh.

NEWSREEL NARRATOR (V.O.) (CONT'D)
It seems everybody these days is rooting for
Roxie Hart.

INT. COOK COUNTY JAIL - ROXIE'S CELL - DAY
A GUARD carries flowers wrapped in yesterday's
papers, with the headline: CONVENT GIRL HELD.

MATRON (O.C.)
Take those wiltin' roses over to the orphanage.
And make sure they know who sent 'em.

The matron moves over to Roxie, who is doodling
in her silver diary. She has her own kimono now.

MATRON (CONT'D)
So, kiddo...you given any thought to what you
wanna do after Billy gets you off?

ROXIE
I think I'd like to go on the stage.

MATRON
I figured as much. I already called the
Morris office.

ROXIE
Really. And how much is that gonna cost me?

MATRON
My standard deal. Ten percent of all your takings.

ROXIE
We'll see, Mama. We'll see.

She sits on her cot. Aloof. The Hunyak passes,
hands Roxie some freshly laundered underwear.

ROXIE (CONT'D)
Besides, I still don't have an act.

MATRON
Killing Fred Casely was your act. That's all
those stiffs in the audience want — to say
they saw somebody famous.

Roxie slips the Hunyak a dollar bill.

ROXIE
That's a freak act. I'm better 'n that.

MATRON
'Course you are, cupcake.

Since shameless flattery comes with the job:

MATRON (CONT'D)
You could be as big as Sophie Tucker. Bigger
than Cantor and Jolson combined.

ROXIE
You think so? You wanna know something,
Mama? I always wanted my name in the
papers. Before Amos, I used to date this
well-to-do ugly bootlegger. He used to like
to take me out and show me off. Ugly guys
like to do that.

The matron opens her mouth to laugh, but we hear
AUDIENCE LAUGHTER instead. We CUT TO:

INT. "STAGE" - NIGHT
Roxie's monologue continues, as a showbiz-fake-
intimate conversation with the audience.

ROXIE
Once it said in the paper, "Gangland's Al Capelli
seen at Chez Vito with cute blonde chorine."
That was me. I clipped it and saved it. See, all
my life I wanted to have my own act. But, no.
No. No. No. They always turned me down. It
was one big world full of "No." Then Amos came
along. Sweet, safe Amos who never says no.

In the crowd, people nod knowingly.

ROXIE (CONT'D)
Look, I've never done this before...but it's such
a special night, and you're such a great audience...I feel like I can really talk to you. So
forget what you've read in the papers or heard
on the radio, 'cause I'm gonna tell you the truth.

The audience glows with gratitude.

Look, I've never done this before...but it's such a special night, and you're such a great audience...I feel like I can really talk to you. So forget what you've read in the papers or heard on the radio, 'cause I'm gonna tell you the truth.

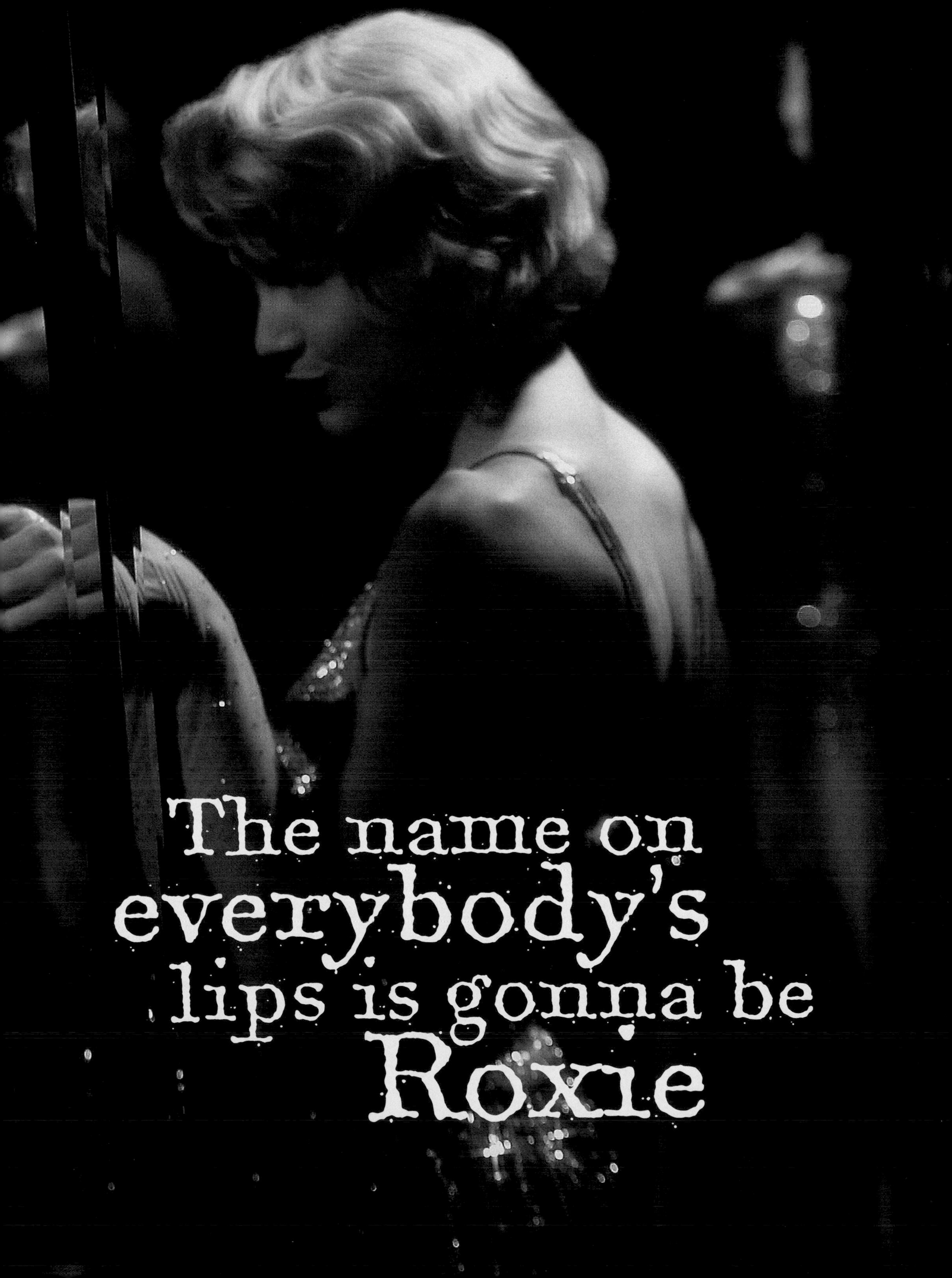

The name on everybody's lips is gonna be Roxie

ROXIE (CONT'D)

Not that the truth really matters, but I'm gonna tell you anyway. In the bed department, Amos was zero. I mean, when he made love to me, it was like he was fixin' a carburetor or somethin'. "I love ya, honey, I love ya."
Anyway, I started foolin' around.
(stands, moves back)
Then I started screwin' around, which is foolin' around without dinner. Then I met Fred Casely, who said he'd get me into vaudeville, but that didn't work out exactly the way I planned. I guess it didn't work out too great for Fred either.

Raucous laughter from the crowd.

INT. VOID SPACE - NIGHT

A black sequined curtain parts behind Roxie.

ROXIE

So I gave up the vaudeville idea, because after all those years...well, you sort of figure opportunity just passed you by. Oh, but it ain't. Oh no, no, no, no, no, it ain't. If this Flynn guy gets me off, and with all this publicity, now, I got me a world full of "Yes."
(sings)
THE NAME ON EVERYBODY'S LIPS
IS GONNA BE ROXIE

A mirror appears. Then another and another, until there are a dozen reflections of Roxie Hart.

ROXIE (CONT'D)
THE LADY RAKIN' IN THE CHIPS
IS GONNA BE ROXIE
I'M GONNA BE A CELEBRITY
THAT MEANS SOMEBODY EVERYONE KNOWS
THEY'RE GONNA RECOGNIZE MY EYES
MY HAIR, MY TEETH, MY BOOBS, MY NOSE
FROM JUST SOME DUMB MECHANIC'S WIFE
I'M GONNA BE ROXIE
WHO SAYS THAT MURDER'S NOT AN ART?
AND WHO IN CASE SHE DOESN'T HANG
CAN SAY SHE STARTED WITH A BANG?
ROXIE HART!

The mirrors rise, revealing a line of men, with another tier of mirrors behind them.

MEN
THEY'RE GONNA WAIT OUTSIDE IN LINE
TO GET TO SEE ROXIE

ROXIE
THINK OF THOSE AUTOGRAPHS I'LL SIGN
"GOOD LUCK TO YOU" ROXIE
AND I'LL APPEAR IN A LAVALIERE
THAT GOES ALL THE WAY DOWN TO
    MY WAIST

The men pull Roxie onto a mirror. It's as though she's making love to herself.

MEN
HERE A RING, THERE A RING
EVERYWHERE A RING A LING

ROXIE
BUT ALWAYS IN THE BEST OF TASTE

A dance break, a display of unbridled adoration of Roxie.

ROXIE (CONT'D)
Mmmm, I'm a star. And the audience loves me and I love them. And they love me for lovin' them and I love them for lovin' me. And we love each other. That's because none of us got enough love in our childhoods. And that's showbiz, kid.

We pull back to see that Roxie and the men are dancing on top of an enormous sign. Just five letters, ROXIE, with a heart dotting the "I."

MEN
SHE'S GIVING UP HER HUMDRUM LIFE

ROXIE
I'M GONNA BE
(speaks)
Sing it!

MEN
ROXIE
SHE MADE A SCANDAL AND A START

ROXIE
AND SOPHIE TUCKER'LL SHIT, I KNOW
TO SEE HER NAME GET BILLED BELOW

ALL
ROXIE HART!

MEN (WHISPERING)
ROXIE! ROXIE! ROXIE! ROCK-SIE! ROXIE! ROXIE!

The sign rises until Roxie disappears from view.

INT. COOK COUNTY JAIL - MATRON'S OFFICE - NIGHT
Velma swoops into the matron's office.

VELMA
Mama, I just can't take it anymore.

The matron is on the phone.

VELMA (CONT'D)
You can't go anywhere without hearing about that dumb tomato....

The matron spins around. She coyly rearranges the triple curls of her blonde Roxie bob.

VELMA (CONT'D)
No, Mama. Not you too.

The matron hangs up the phone.

MATRON
I got some bad news, kid. The tour's been cancelled.

VELMA
What?

MATRON
Your name's been out of the papers too long. All you read about today is that Hart kid. She's hot.

VELMA
So what am I supposed to do? Suck up to her like everybody else?

MATRON
It couldn't hurt.

VELMA
Over my dead body.

INT. COOK COUNTY JAIL - COMMON ROOM - NIGHT
Roxie is sitting alone at a table, her clippings spread in front of her. The room is dark, just a dim light bulb and the moonlight streaming through the window.

VELMA (O.S.)
Mind if I join you?

Roxie looks up, sees Velma smiling sweetly. A VOICE crackles on the PA system.

GUARD'S VOICE
Lights out in ten minutes.

Velma takes out a pack of cigarettes.

VELMA
Smoke?

Roxie holds up the one she's already got going.

VELMA (CONT'D)
Look what some Johnny sent me. Triple cream caramels all the way from San Francisco.

She offers the candies to Roxie, who smiles demurely.

ROXIE
I'm watching my figure. You know, the trial...

Velma swallows hard, stifling the urge to kill.

VELMA
Great mention of you in the *Trib* today.

ROXIE
There's been so many, I can't keep track.

VELMA
Hey, did I ever tell you that you're exactly the same size as my sister? You'd fit into her costumes perfectly.

ROXIE
Really?

She sticks out her tongue and runs it down the back of a clipping.

VELMA
I was thinking, you know...with all the publicity that's piled up between us, when Billy gets us off, we'd be a natural to do an act together.

ROXIE
You think so?

The shrill blast of a siren. The prison searchlights begin to rotate in the yard, as the BANDLEADER's muffled voice interrupts on the PA system:

BANDLEADER (V.O.)
Ladies and gentlemen, Miss Velma Kelly in an act of desperation.

The searchlights lock into place, forming a shaft of light which shines through the windows.

INT. FANTASY COMMON ROOM - NIGHT
Velma steps into the dirty spot.

VELMA
MY SISTER AND I HAD AN ACT THAT
    COULDN'T FLOP
MY SISTER AND I WERE HEADED
    STRAIGHT FOR THE TOP
MY SISTER AND I EARNED A THOU A
    WEEK AT LEAST
BUT MY SISTER IS NOW,
    UNFORTUNATELY, DECEASED
I KNOW, IT'S SAD, OF COURSE, BUT A
    FACT IS STILL A FACT
AND NOW ALL THAT REMAINS
IS THE REMAINS OF A PERFECT
    DOUBLE ACT!

Velma grabs the newspaper from Roxie, throws it on the table.

First I'd...
Then she'd...
Then we'd...
But I can't do it alone!
Then she'd...
Then I'd...
Then we'd...
But I can't do it alone!

VELMA (CONT'D)
Watch this.

She drops her robe, revealing a red costume studded
with rhinestones. The pipes lining the wall glow with
light, creating a proscenium frame behind Velma.

VELMA (CONT'D)
Now, you have to imagine it with two people.
It's swell with two people.
(sings)
FIRST I'D...
THEN SHE'D...
THEN WE'D...
BUT I CAN'T DO IT ALONE!
THEN SHE'D...
THEN I'D...
THEN WE'D...
BUT I CAN'T DO IT ALONE!
SHE'D SAY, "WHAT'S YOUR SISTER LIKE?"
I'D SAY, "MEN,"
SHE'D SAY, "YOU'RE THE CAT'S MEOW"
THEN WE'D WOW THE CROWD AGAIN
WHEN SHE'D GO...
I'D GO...
WE'D GO...

AND THEN THOSE DING DONG DADDIES
    STARTED TO ROAR
WHISTLED, STOMPED, AND STAMPED
    ON THE FLOOR
YELLING, SCREAMING, BEGGING FOR MORE
(speaks)
And we'd say, "O.K. fellas, keep your socks up.
You ain't seen nothin' yet!"

VELMA (CONT'D)
BUT I SIMPLY CANNOT DO IT ALONE

Velma gives it the big finish, landing on the floor
across from Roxie. A moment later...

INT. COOK COUNTY JAIL - COMMON ROOM - NIGHT
We're back to reality. Velma once again sits
opposite Roxie, whose face is still buried in the
newspaper.

VELMA
So what do you think? Come on, you can say.

Roxie gives her a raspberry.

VELMA (CONT'D)
I know, you're right, the first part's shit, but
the second part is really nifty.

INT. FANTASY COMMON ROOM - NIGHT
MUSIC and LIGHTS come up again. Velma takes the cigarette from Roxie's lips, stubs it out.

> **VELMA**
> Okay.
> (sings)
> SHE'D GO...
> I'D GO...
> WE'D GO...
> AND THEN THOSE TWO-BIT JOHNNIES
> DID IT UP BROWN
> TO CHEER THE BEST ATTRACTION IN TOWN
> THEY NEARLY TORE THE BALCONY DOWN

She climbs the stairs.

> **VELMA** (CONT'D)
> And we'd say, "You know what, boys, we're going home. But before we go, here's a few more partin' shots!" And this...this we did in perfect unison.

Velma dances on the landing.

> **VELMA** (CONT'D)
> NOW YOU'VE SEEN ME GOING THROUGH IT
> (climbs over a railing)
> IT MAY SEEM THERE'S NOTHIN' TO IT
> BUT I SIMPLY CANNOT DO IT

She grabs hold of a pole and slides down.

> **VELMA** (CONT'D)
> ALONE!

Velma glides on her stomach across the table, ending just in front of Roxie.

INT. COOK COUNTY JAIL - COMMON ROOM - NIGHT
Roxie looks over to Velma, who is sitting in her original position again.

> **ROXIE**
> So where's the part where you blew her brains out?

> **VELMA**
> Okay, Roxie, I'll level with you...

> **ROXIE**
> Don't bother. You think you're foolin' me?

She collects her things.

> **ROXIE** (CONT'D)
> You're all washed up. It's me they want now. I'm a big star — single.

She stands.

> **ROXIE** (CONT'D)
> Oh, I almost forgot. You were in the paper today, too.

She rifles through the stack of articles, finds the tiniest clipping.

> **ROXIE** (CONT'D)
> In the back. With the obituaries.

She squints at the clipping.

> **ROXIE** (CONT'D)
> "Velma Kelly's trial has been postponed. Indefinitely."
> (counts on her fingers)
> Seven words. Wow.

On the way out:

> **ROXIE** (CONT'D)
> Oh, and here's a piece of advice, direct from me to you. Lay off the caramels.

She leaves, slamming the door behind her. Velma gazes out at the prison searchlight. It sweeps across the yard...

> **BANDLEADER** (V.O.)
> And now for all you Chicago stay-up-laters...

EXT. CHICAGO SKYLINE - NIGHT (LATER)
...and brings us to the glittering skyline.

> **BANDLEADER** (V.O.)
> ...you night owls who only come alive after dark...

INT. THE ONYX - NIGHT
The BANDLEADER intones into a radio microphone:

> **BANDLEADER**
> ...we dedicate this next tune, "Chicago After Midnight."

The band starts to play on the thrust. Tables have been cleared to create a space for COUPLES to dance.

INT. COOK COUNTY JAIL - ROXIE'S CELL - NIGHT
Roxie listens to the radio in her cell. She writes in her silver diary.

INT. PUMP ROOM - NIGHT
The walls are covered with framed photographs of celebrities. Baseball players, movie stars, gangsters — and Billy Flynn. We pan down from Billy's

picture to the man himself. A telephone has been brought to the table.

> **BILLY**
> ...and all that happened on Lakeshore Drive? Incredible.

Billy hangs up, repeats the story to the other people at the table:

> **BILLY** (CONT'D)
> They just arrested a woman for triple homicide. And get this — she's an heiress! Her folks are in pineapples, grapefruits, some kind of fruit. Anyway, this dame, Kitty something-or-other, she's playing house on the North Side with a guy named Harry...

INT. LAKESHORE DRIVE APARTMENT - NIGHT
KITTY BAXTER, a beautiful woman in her middle 20s, enters the apartment and moves toward the bedroom.

> **BILLY** (V.O.)
> What Harry does for a living nobody is quite sure, but it don't matter because she's footing all the bills. Anyhow, Kitty comes home tonight

and Harry's already in bed — which is par for the course for Harry.

Kitty passes the bed, sees Harry sprawled under the covers.

> **BILLY** (V.O.) (CONT'D)
> She goes to change...and when she returns she notices something rather odd. Extremely odd.

Back in the bedroom, Kitty notices a third arm hanging from the bed. She moves to the other side, sees yet another pair of feet sticking out from under the sheets.

> **BILLY** (V.O.) (CONT'D)
> Kitty disappears for a second. Cool as a cucumber.

Kitty hyperventilates, deeply upset. She moves toward the closet.

> **BILLY** (V.O.) (CONT'D)
> When she returns she gently wakes up Harry...

Kitty emerges with a gun. She pulls off the covers, revealing two naked women in bed with Harry. They all scream.

INT. THE PUMP ROOM - NIGHT
Billy finishes the story.

> **BILLY**
> So the husband says, "What? I'm alone."
> "Alone?" she says. "You got two other women
> in bed with you."

INT. LAKESHORE DRIVE APARTMENT - NIGHT
One of the women jumps up and covers herself
with the drapes, while the other reaches for a pillow. Harry lifts his hands and bursts into tears.

INT. THE PUMP ROOM - NIGHT
Billy can hardly get the words out, he's laughing
so hard.

> **BILLY**
> Now get this. Harry says, "Come on, doll.
> Are you gonna believe what you see or what
> I tell you?"

The table explodes in laughter.

INT. LAKESHORE DRIVE APARTMENT - NIGHT
Kitty sprays the mattress with bullets. Harry and
the woman behind the pillow die a quick, brutal
death.

The other woman cowers in the corner, begging for

her life. Kitty aims and shoots. The woman dies in
slow motion, as if she's dancing to the band.

INT. THE ONYX - NIGHT
The BANDLEADER leans into the microphone.

> **BANDLEADER**
> Goodnight, folks.

The MUSIC ends.

EXT. COOK COUNTY JAIL - DAY
A GUARD paces the perimeter wall, drenched by a
pounding rain. Below him, we see dozens of bobbing umbrellas, as reporters and photographers
rush to surround Kitty and Billy.

INT. COOK COUNTY JAIL - HALLWAY - DAY
The matron and several guards escort a soaked
Kitty into jail, accompanied by Billy and the press
horde. She's a reluctant heroine, kicking at the
men trying to take her picture.

The throng moves past the cell block common area,
where Roxie, Velma, and several other inmates
watch them pass.

> **BILLY**
> Please direct your questions to her counsel.

KITTY
You're not my counsel, and I want my money back.

BILLY
It's not your money, it's your mother's money.

[Roxie tries to catch Mary Sunshine's attention, but she seems uninterested]

The reporters file past without even a glance in Roxie's direction.

REPORTER #1
Miss Baxter, did you know these two ladies personally?

KITTY (SMILING)
Did I know these two ladies personally? Was that your question?

REPORTER #1
Yes, that's my question.

Kitty knees him in the groin. The matron motions for the guard to subdue her.

MATRON
Oh, she's very high spirited, isn't she?

Roxie moves to the end of the common room, calls out to Billy through the bars.

ROXIE
Mr. Flynn! Mr. Flynn!

BILLY
Hi, Trixie.

ROXIE
It's Roxie.

BILLY
Of course, I was just kidding.

ROXIE
Did you get my trial date yet?

BILLY
Listen, kid...

ROXIE
I know, I'm at the top of your list.

BILLY (LOOKING PAST HER)
Boy, what a hellion, huh? And a socialite, too! Her mother owns all the pineapples in Hawaii.

ROXIE
What the hell do I care about pineapples?

He turns back to the reporters.

BILLY
Miss Baxter will answer all your questions and afterwards I'll be happy to give you an interview myself...

Roxie takes a few steps back.

INT. "STAGE" - NIGHT
On the stage, the "ROXIE" sign goes dark.

INT. COOK COUNTY JAIL - DAY
Velma steps up to Roxie.

VELMA
How's it feel, kid?

She holds up the morning papers, which are filled with stories about the Lakeshore Drive Massacre.

VELMA (CONT'D)
J. Edgar Hoover couldn't find your name in the papers.

She drops the papers in Roxie's hand and starts off. Roxie gives a sudden shriek and crumbles in a faint. She moans, with eyes closed, then lifts her head a little to call out:

ROXIE
Mr. Flynn? Miss Sunshine?

She faints again. The reporters make a beeline for Roxie. Mary Sunshine peers down at her through the open bars.

MARY SUNSHINE
What is it, dear?

Billy turns to a guard, gestures grandly for the cameras.

BILLY
Someone unlock that door immediately.

ROXIE (WAN AND SWEET)
Oh, don't worry about...me. I just hope the fall didn't hurt the baby!

MATRON
Baby!

Roxie nods solemnly.

VELMA
Shit.

Roxie and Velma exchange looks. Flashbulbs pop

and peppy MUSIC plays ("Me and My Baby") as we CUT TO:

EXT. CHICAGO STREETS - DAY

A police escort leads a prison ambulance through midday traffic.

INT. COUNTY HOSPITAL - DAY

A nebbishy DOCTOR steps out of the examining room, his face flushed. Behind him, we can see Roxie pulling on her prison uniform.

> **BILLY**
>
> Well, Doc, is she or isn't she?

> **DOCTOR**
>
> She is.

Billy puts his arm around the doctor.

> **BILLY**
>
> Would you swear to that statement in court?

> **DOCTOR**
>
> Yes.

> **BILLY**
>
> Good...uh...button your fly.

EXT. COUNTY HOSPITAL - DAY

Snow blankets the street as the matron pushes Roxie's wheelchair through the front doors. There is an immediate crush of reporters and cameras.

> **REPORTERS** (OVERLAPPING)
>
> Roxie, how ya feelin'? When's the baby due? How long have you known, Roxie?

[Roxie says that she doesn't care what happens to her; all that matters is the life of her unborn child.]

Behind the reporters, we see Amos jump off a streetcar.

> **BILLY**
>
> I can assure you she'll come to trial at the earliest possible moment. And you can quote me on that.

> **MATRON**
>
> I think it's sweet. First time we ever had one of our girls knocked up.

> **AMOS**
>
> Hey Roxie, I just heard the good news!

He tries to push his way through the crowd.

Lucy Liu

As the hellcat heiress Kitty Baxter, Lucy Liu says she "wreaks havoc for a bit, and then goes away." And although it's a relatively small role, Liu makes it a juicy, memorable one.

Kitty "finds her husband in bed with two other women and decides that she needs to take care of business immediately, so she murders them," Liu says.

"She's very wealthy, so she can pretty much do anything she wants, and her father is always taking care of her. But this time she's gotten herself in a situation that might be a little more difficult," Liu adds with understatement.

Kitty certainly could use an anger-management class, and she tells off the reporters and even her attorney, Billy Flynn, who can't seem to resist defending yet another beautiful murderess.

But Liu's Kitty isn't just a drama queen, she's also dramatically crucial to *Chicago*'s story. When she steals the headlines away from Roxie, who had been basking in her newfound celebrity, Roxie realizes the transience of her fame. It's no coincidence that just when all of the reporters are ignoring her for the latest jailhouse beauty, Roxie announces that she's pregnant.

"But being the way I am helps to propel the rest of the movie and to explain why Roxie makes the decisions that she does," Liu says.

Liu also sees her role as distilling the essence of *Chicago*'s story. "It's about women, women committing crimes—crimes of the heart, or crimes of jealousy, of rage. So mix that with music and dance, and I think that you can't go wrong."

AMOS (CONT'D)

I'm the father! I'm the father!

[A reporter inquires about the child's paternity.]

BILLY

That question is completely out of line.

He puts a protective arm around Roxie.

BILLY (CONT'D)

That's enough for now. My client needs her rest.

Billy opens the ambulance doors.

AMOS

Roxie! Rox, it's me! Daddy.

EXT. STREET - DAY

Amos steps back on the sidewalk, turns to people walking by.

AMOS

Roxie, I came as soon as I could!

MUSIC starts under.

INT. AMBULANCE - DAY

Roxie gazes out at Amos, a look of pity in her eyes.

AMOS (V.O.)

IF SOMEONE STOOD UP IN A CROWD

AND RAISED HIS VOICE UP WAY OUT LOUD
AND WAVED HIS ARM
AND SHOOK HIS LEG
YOU'D NOTICE HIM

From Roxie's POV, we see Amos standing alone in the snow.

INT. "STAGE" - NIGHT

We move down a smoke-filled shaft of light, then slowly across the surface of a make-up table. Amos's hands apply bits of make-up, rouge and eyeliner.

AMOS (O.C.)

IF SOMEONE IN A MOVIE SHOW
YELLED "FIRE IN THE SECOND ROW,
THIS WHOLE PLACE IS A POWDER KEG!"
YOU'D NOTICE HIM

Amos reaches for unseen items of clothing and pulls them on.

AMOS (O.C.) (CONT'D)

AND EVEN WITHOUT CLUCKING
LIKE A HEN
EVERYONE GETS NOTICED
NOW AND THEN

> UNLESS OF COURSE THAT PERSONAGE
> SHOULD BE
> INVISIBLE, INCONSEQUENTIAL ME!

Amos turns and stands. He is dressed as a stage tramp, in a cellophane coat, top hat, and oversized shoes. The table slides off, revealing the bare brick wall of the theater.

AMOS (CONT'D)
CELLOPHANE
MISTER CELLOPHANE
SHOULD HAVE BEEN MY NAME
MISTER CELLOPHANE
'CAUSE YOU CAN LOOK RIGHT THROUGH ME
WALK RIGHT BY ME
AND NEVER KNOW I'M THERE!

There's hardly anyone in the club, and the ones who are there aren't paying attention. Amos' shadow looms on the wall behind him.

AMOS (CONT'D)
I TELL YA
CELLOPHANE
MISTER CELLOPHANE
SHOULD HAVE BEEN MY NAME
MISTER CELLOPHANE
'CAUSE YOU CAN LOOK RIGHT THROUGH ME
WALK RIGHT BY ME
AND NEVER KNOW I'M THERE....

Amos takes off his hat.

INT. BILLY FLYNN'S OFFICE - DAY
Billy is seated behind his desk, reading a paper. Amos stands opposite him, hat in hand. He coughs softly.

BILLY
Oh, I didn't see you. Sit down. Sit down. Look, Andy, I'm afraid I gotta hit you hard. I can only hope you'll be big about it.

AMOS (SLIGHTLY IRRITATED)
Amos. My name is Amos.

BILLY
Who said it wasn't? It's the kid's name I'm thinkin' about. You know when she's due? September.

A look of confusion crosses Amos' face.

BILLY
Can you count? September?

Cellophane
Mister Cellophane
Should have been my name
Mister cellophane
'cause you can look right
through me
Walk right by me
And never know
I'm there!

He takes out a piece of paper.

BILLY (CONT'D)
Here's a copy of Roxie's first statement, from the D.A.'s office. It says she hadn't copulated with you for four months prior to...the incident.

AMOS
Well she would know. I guess we hadn't done no copulating since...now, wait a minute.

He has his head back, eyes on ceiling, lost in calculation.

AMOS (CONT'D)
...that don't figure out right. I couldn't be the father.

BILLY
Forget all that now. My client needs your support.

AMOS (ANGER BUILDING)
This time...this time she's gone too far.

AMOS (CONT'D)
I'll divorce her.
(after a beat)
She probably won't even notice.

The intercom buzzes and Billy picks up the phone.

BILLY
Put him through.

Billy picks up the phone. He glances at Amos.

BILLY (CONT'D)
You still here, Andy?

He hands Amos his hat.

AMOS
Yeah, I'm still here. I think.

Amos takes the hat...

INT. "STAGE" - NIGHT
...and puts on the cellophane hat.

AMOS
A HUMAN BEING'S MADE OF MORE THAN AIR
WITH ALL THAT BULK, YOU'RE BOUND TO
   SEE HIM THERE
UNLESS THAT HUMAN BEIN' NEXT TO YOU
IS UNIMPRESSIVE, UNDISTINGUISHED
   YOU KNOW WHO...

Amos seems to shrink as the oppressive shadow grows behind him.

AMOS (CONT'D)
SHOULD HAVE BEEN MY NAME
MISTER CELLOPHANE
'CAUSE YOU CAN LOOK RIGHT THROUGH ME
WALK RIGHT BY ME
AND NEVER KNOW I'M THERE...

His singing is powerful and raw. All that resentment and rage finally bursting through.

AMOS (CONT'D)
I TELL YA
CELLOPHANE
MISTER CELLOPHANE
SHOULD HAVE BEEN MY NAME
MISTER CELLOPHANE
'CAUSE YOU CAN LOOK RIGHT THROUGH ME
WALK RIGHT BY ME
AND NEVER KNOW I'M THERE
NEVER EVEN KNOW...

Amos catches himself, surprised by his own ferocity.

AMOS (CONT'D)
...I'M THERE

INT. BILLY'S OFFICE - DAY
Amos turns back to Billy, tilts his head apologetically.

AMOS
Hope I didn't take up too much of your time.

Amos shuts the door, as MUSIC ends.

INT. COOK COUNTY JAIL - HOLDING ROOM - DAY
Another door opens and Roxie appears, holding up a dress with lace around the neck and sleeves. A star who hates her costume.

BILLY
I've been waiting here for ten minutes. Don't do that again.

ROXIE
This dress makes me look like a Woolworth's lamp shade. I'm not wearing it.

BILLY
You're wearing it because I tell you to wear it. And when Andy is on the stand, I want you to be knitting.

ROXIE
Knitting?

John C. Reilly

John C. Reilly, who plays Amos Hart, is quick to point out that he's the only actor in the cast of *Chicago* who was born and raised in the Windy City. Then he's quick to point out that it doesn't really matter. "This is not really a movie about Chicago, even though it's called *Chicago*," he explains. "It just so happens that in its day at this time in the '20s, this is what the world was like there."

Instead, Reilly sees the story as universal. "It has this timeless feel. It's about celebrity, how people become famous. It's almost like it doesn't matter what you do to become famous. Once you become famous, that's good enough. Soak it up and get your book deal or your talk show or whatever."

Perhaps more relevant to this production is the musical theater Reilly did while coming of age in Chicago. "As a kid, I had done a lot of musicals because that's all there was to do where I grew up," he says. "No one really did straight plays, you know, it was all community theater, and all the shows I did in high school were musicals."

"I think in these times of crises, people want to be encouraged to have hope, and the musicals are full of hope. There's just something really pure about someone singing, and telling a story by singing."

Nevertheless, Reilly believes director Rob Marshall chose him on the basis of his movie roles not his musical experience. "As Amos, I'm married to Roxie, a very ambitious wannabe showgirl, and I'm just a simple mechanic who loves her," he explains. "I suppose he's really a victim of love. I think there's often people like that behind very ambitious people, people who just love them unconditionally and see something in them that maybe they don't even realize themselves. I always end up playing characters like that—people either totally deluded, or completely naïve, or just dreamers somehow. I suppose I'm a little bit like that."

But the poignance of Reilly's rendition of "Mr. Cellophane" proves that he does have the soul of a singer. And he believes in the relevance of musicals today. "I think in these times of crises, people want to be encouraged to have hope, and the musicals are full of hope. There's just something really pure about someone singing, and telling a story by singing."

BILLY
A baby garment.

ROXIE
Oh, for Chrissakes. I don't know how to knit.

BILLY
Well, learn.

ROXIE
That's no way to get a jury's sympathy.

BILLY
Oh, now you don't need any advice.

She picks up a tabloid — the headline reads 'ROXIE TO D.A.: DON'T HANG MY BABY' — and throws it at him.

ROXIE
Lookit here, Mr. Mouthpiece, it seems to me that I'm the one coming up with all the good ideas.
(a street fighter — tough)
I am sick of everybody tellin' me what to do. You treat me like dirt, Billy Flynn. Like some dumb, common criminal.

BILLY
But you are some dumb, common criminal.

ROXIE (YELLING)
That's better than bein' a greasy Mick lawyer.

BILLY (YELLING BACK)
Who happens to be saving your ass!

ROXIE
Who's out for all he can steal!

BILLY
Oh, maybe you'd like to appear in court without me.

ROXIE
Maybe I could. Have you read the morning papers? They love me.

BILLY
Wise up. They'd love you a lot more if you were hanged. You know why? Because it would sell more papers.

ROXIE
You're fired!

BILLY
I quit.

He shuts his briefcase.

ROXIE
Any lawyer in this town would die to have my case!

BILLY
You're a phony celebrity. A flash-in-the-pan. In a couple of weeks, no one's gonna give a shit about you. That's Chicago.

He slams the door.

INT. COOK COUNTY JAIL - CORRIDOR - DAY (CONTINUOUS)
As Roxie heads back to her cell, Annie runs past her.

ROXIE
What's goin' on?

Roxie follows Annie into the block, where several inmates are huddled.

VELMA
It's the Hunyak. She lost her last appeal.

Across the way, the Hunyak is led back to her cell by the matron.

ROXIE
So what's that mean?

VELMA (NODS)
Next week she's gonna...

She grabs her neck, as if she's being hanged.

INT. COOK COUNTY JAIL - HUNYAK'S CELL - DAY
The Hunyak makes the sign of the cross.

INT. "STAGE" - DRESSING ROOM - DAY
The Hunyak, wearing a sexy leotard, pats her face, chest and shoulders with a powder puff.

EXT. COOK COUNTY JAIL - DAY
Mary Sunshine files a radio report from the prison. There are protesters gathered outside the gates.

MARY SUNSHINE
This is Mary Sunshine coming to you from the Cook County Jail, where history will be made today. Katalin Halenscki will become the first woman in the state of Illinois to be executed. And so, ladies and gentlemen...

INT. "STAGE" - NIGHT
Mary Sunshine's voice cross-fades to the band-leader, who stands in the orchestra pit:

BANDLEADER
...and now, ladies and gentlemen, for your pleasure and your entertainment, we proudly present...the one...the only Katalin Halenscki and her famous Hungarian disappearing act.

A drum roll...

EXT. COOK COUNTY JAIL - INNER YARD - DAY
...which continues as glum-faced WITNESSES file into position opposite the gallows. Assistant D.A. HARRISON takes his place in front.

INT. "STAGE" - NIGHT
The audience waits in silent anticipation.

EXT. COOK COUNTY JAIL - INNER YARD - DAY
The Hunyak climbs a set of steep narrow stairs behind the gallows.

INT. "STAGE" - NIGHT
The Hunyak climbs a ladder on the stage.

EXT. COOK COUNTY JAIL - INNER YARD - DAY
The hanging witnesses watch soberly. A GUARD places a noose around the Hunyak's neck.

INT. "STAGE" - NIGHT
The Hunyak steps onto a platform fifteen feet above the stage. She steps into a rope and tightens it around her waist.

EXT. COOK COUNTY JAIL - INNER YARD - DAY
The Hunyak trembles as the guard positions her feet over the trap door.

INT. "STAGE" - NIGHT
The Hunyak tests the edge of the platform with her foot. The audience leans forward in suspense and delight...

EXT. COOK COUNTY JAIL - INNER YARD - DAY
The guard pulls back on a wooden lever. The floor drops away and the Hunyak starts to fall.

INT. "STAGE" - NIGHT
The Hunyak pushes off, starting a graceful swan dive. It's as if she's taking off for freedom.

EXT. COOK COUNTY JAIL - INNER YARD - DAY
The Hunyak continues to fall.

INT. "STAGE" - NIGHT
The stage is filled with an explosion of white smoke, from which a dozen white DOVES emerge, wings fluttering. The Hunyak is gone, leaving an empty rope swinging in her place.

EXT. COOK COUNTY JAIL - INNER YARD - DAY

A few witnesses cover their eyes. Harrison nods, satisfied that justice has been served. The Hunyak's body twists slowly on the rope.

INT. "STAGE" - NIGHT

The audience goes wild with applause.

INT. COOK COUNTY JAIL - DAY (LATER)

Through a window, Roxie sees the Hunyak's body carried across the yard on a covered stretcher. She stifles a sob, as we FADE OUT.

INT. COOK COUNTY COURTHOUSE - PRISONER'S ROOM - DAY

A dingy room, with high brown walls that are beginning to scale off. Roxie wears the frilly dress she hated before. She looks in the mirror, rearranges the lace around her neck.

> **ROXIE**
> You know, it's not really that bad.

Billy hands her the knitting.

> **BILLY**
> Now you're clear about everything?

> **ROXIE**
> Yeah, I been up all night rehearsing.

> **BILLY**
> And what do you do when Harrison starts coming after you?

> **ROXIE**
> I sit still and look straight ahead. Never at the jury.

> **BILLY**
> And?

> **ROXIE**
> And I look modest.

Roxie attempts modest.

> **BILLY**
> And?

> **ROXIE**
> And...

> **BILLY**
> And say nothing! That was the deal, right? I do all the talking this time.

> **ROXIE**
> Absolutely, Billy. Whatever you say.

The BAILIFF knocks and enters.

> **BAILIFF**
> Mr. Flynn, His Honor is here.

> **BILLY** (QUIETLY)
> Thank you. You ready?

> **ROXIE**
> Yeah. Billy...

He turns.

> **ROXIE** (CONT'D)
> I'm scared.

Billy smiles, gentle for the first time.

> **BILLY**
> Don't be. I've been around a long time, and believe me, you got nothin' to worry about. It's all a circus.

He takes her hand, gentle for the first time. MUSIC starts under.

> **BILLY** (CONT'D)
> A three-ring circus. These trials — the whole world — all show business. But kid, you're working with a star.

Billy starts to open the door.

> **BILLY** (CONT'D)
> GIVE 'EM THE OLD RAZZLE DAZZLE

INT. FANTASY COURTROOM - NIGHT

Two ethereal SHOWGIRLS pull the doors open. Billy and Roxie enter the courtroom, where familiar elements — the judge's bench, the jury box, the witness stand — surround a center ring. Two other SHOWGIRLS cross the aisle, while another PAIR pull a diaphanous tent around the perimeter.

> **BILLY**
> RAZZLE DAZZLE 'EM

Billy and Roxie move up the aisle. Another SHOWGIRL descends like a chandelier, lush fabrics swooping from her spinning figure.

> **BILLY** (CONT'D)
> GIVE 'EM AN ACT WITH LOTS OF FLASH IN IT

Two female CONTORTIONISTS do back walk-overs on the defense and prosecution tables. Billy rotates Roxie, shows her the SPECTATORS applauding in slow motion.

BILLY (CONT'D)
AND THE REACTION WILL BE PASSIONATE

Billy backs up. Two more dazzling SHOWGIRLS descend on long silks, hanging upside down.

BILLY (CONT'D)
GIVE 'EM THE OLD HOCUS POCUS
BEAD AND FEATHER 'EM
HOW CAN THEY SEE WITH SEQUINS
    IN THEIR EYES?

The showgirls toss sequins in unison. Billy leads Roxie through the gate, as one of the girls slips him a Bible.

BILLY (CONT'D)
WHAT IF YOUR HINGES ALL ARE RUSTING?

Billy lounges on the defense table, cigar in one hand, Bible in the other, posing for a picture.

BILLY (CONT'D)
WHAT IF, IN FACT, YOU'RE JUST DISGUSTING?

Billy deposits the cigar in a showgirl's mouth. He leads Roxie to the photographers, puts the Bible in her hand.

BILLY (CONT'D)
RAZZLE DAZZLE 'EM
AND THEY'LL NEVER CATCH WISE!

INT. COURTROOM - DAY (BACK TO REALITY)
MUSIC continues under as Billy poses with Roxie, who is holding a Bible. A dozen newspaper PHO-TOGRAPHERS lean out from the press bleachers.

PHOTOGRAPHERS (ALL AT ONCE)
Hey, Billy! Roxie! Make it pretty, Rox! Up here, Billy! C'mon, smile for the camera!

Billy and Roxie offer their best profiles and adopt appropriately sober expressions. Behind them, Harrison sits at the prosecution table, seething.

INT. FANTASY COURTROOM - NIGHT
Billy jumps onto the stenographer's desk. A blind-folded TRAPEZE ARTIST rises from behind the judge's bench, sitting on the scales of Justice.

BILLY
GIVE 'EM THE OLD RAZZLE DAZZLE

WOMEN
RAZZLE DAZZLE 'EM

Two other showgirls open the tent and the JUDGE appears. The women accompany him to his bench.

BILLY
GIVE 'EM A SHOW THAT'S SO SPLENDIFEROUS

The BAILIFF stands on the witness chair and prompts the court to rise for the judge, while two showgirls cross with handwritten 'APPLAUSE' signs.

BILLY (CONT'D)
ROW AFTER ROW WILL GROW VOCIFEROUS

Everyone stands and cheers. Billy jumps off the desk and crosses to the judge. An apple drops from the chandelier.

BILLY (CONT'D)
GIVE 'EM THE OLD FLIM FLAM FLUMMOX

A showgirl splays herself on the judge's bench. Billy polishes the apple and perches it on her belly button.

BILLY (CONT'D)
FOOL AND FRACTURE 'EM

The judge bobs for the apple, as Billy grabs the Bible from Roxie and backs up toward the jury box.

BILLY (CONT'D)
HOW CAN THEY HEAR THE TRUTH ABOVE THE ROAR?

He swings around to face the jury.

INT. COURTROOM - DAY (REALITY)
Billy makes a thunderous opening statement. He slams the Bible on the railing, causing the jurors to jump.

WOMEN (V.O.)
ROAR. ROAR.

INT. FANTASY COURTROOM - NIGHT
Five showgirls rise behind the jurors and whisper in their ears.

WOMEN
ROAR.

Billy startles Harrison by pretending to throw the Bible at him. Instead he tosses it to the bailiff, who calls Sgt. Fogarty to the stand.

BILLY
THROW 'EM A FAKE AND A FINAGLE

Billy jumps onto the defense table. He's made it all the way around the courtroom.

BILLY (CONT'D)
THEY'LL NEVER KNOW, YOU'RE JUST A BAGEL

Sgt. Fogarty takes the stand. Billy straddles the defense and prosecution tables, forcing Harrison to pass under his crotch.

BILLY & WOMEN
RAZZLE DAZZLE 'EM

Sgt. Fogarty places his hand on the Bible. The bailiff swears him in.

BILLY
AND THEY'LL BEG YOU FOR MORE!

Before Harrison can get out the first question, Billy jumps off the table.

INT. COURTROOM - DAY (REALITY)
Billy leaps out of his chair. MUSIC continues under.

BILLY
I object!

HARRISON
Your Honor, I haven't even asked the question yet.

JUDGE
Sustained.

Harrison shakes his head in frustration.

INT. FANTASY COURTROOM - NIGHT
Billy stands by the jury box, surrounded by showgirls. They each hold up a different number of fingers.

INT. COURTROOM - DAY (REALITY)
MUSIC continues, as Mrs. Borusewicz squints and lowers her glasses. At the jury box, Billy holds up three fingers. Mrs. Borusewicz turns to the judge, shrugs in confusion.

Billy throws a knowing look at the jurors.

INT. FANTASY COURTROOM - NIGHT
A TRAPEZE ARTIST swings gracefully in front of Billy.

BILLY
GIVE 'EM THE OLD RAZZLE DAZZLE RAZZLE DAZZLE 'EM

She drops the tagged murder weapon into Billy's hands.

INT. COURTROOM - DAY (REALITY)
A reenactment of the crime. Billy plays Roxie, while his huge barrel-chested ASSISTANT portrays

"It's all a circus. A three-ring circus. These trials—the whole world—all show business."

—BILLY FLYNN

"**B**eing on the courtroom set was really amazing because that sequence is exactly as you see it. We stood in that space as it transformed in front of our eyes from a courtroom into this fantastic circus. And we stood there as these beautiful girls fell out of the sky throwing sequins. It was as magical, even more magical if you can imagine physically being there on the set. It was so much fun because the grips and electricians and drivers and all of these people would just sit back with these big grins on their faces. They would be seeing these enormous long production numbers for the first time and just having a blast."

—JOHN MYHRE, PRODUCTION DESIGNER

ABOVE: Rob Marshall on the courtroom set.

a brutish Fred Casely. They both reach for the gun on the defense table, as Roxie watches, trembling.

> BILLY (V.O.)
> BACK SINCE THE DAYS OF OLD METHUSALEH

Billy gets hold of the gun, closes his eyes and shoots three times. Roxie opens her mouth in horror.

> BILLY (V.O.) (CONT'D)
> EVERYONE LOVES THE BIG BAMBOOZ-A-LER

The assistant drops to the floor, filling the taped outline of Casely's body.

INT. FANTASY COURTROOM - NIGHT
A showgirl rearranges the assistant's hand so that it fits within the lines. Billy stands on a chair in the center ring, as eight showgirls parade large pieces of evidence in front of the jury. The layout of the apartment...a photograph of the crime scene...the fingerprints on the gun...a medical drawing of the bullet wounds...Roxie's phone records...even Casely's blood-encrusted clothes.

> BILLY
> GIVE 'EM THE OLD THREE-RING CIRCUS
> STUN AND STAGGER 'EM

Billy picks up the chair and uses it to keep the jurors in line, while eight other showgirls dance behind him.

> BILLY (CONT'D)
> WHEN YOU'RE IN TROUBLE, GO INTO
>   YOUR DANCE

INT. COURTROOM - DAY (REALITY)
Amos has just been called to the stand. He walks past Roxie, who reaches out to him.

> BILLY (V.O.)
> THOUGH YOU ARE STIFFER THAN A GIRDER

Amos snubs Roxie. Billy rests a consoling hand on her shoulder.

> BILLY (V.O.) (CONT'D)
> THEY'LL LET YOU GET AWAY WITH
>   MURDER

INT. FANTASY COURTROOM - NIGHT
Billy gives Roxie a quick spin, then sits her down.

> BILLY
> RAZZLE DAZZLE 'EM
> AND YOU'VE GOT A ROMANCE

Billy moves over to the witness stand. Behind him, the two spinning circus girls rise to the ceiling.

INT. COURTROOM - DAY (REALITY)
MUSIC continues under as Billy smiles pleasantly at Amos.

> BILLY
> Hello, Amos.

Amos is amazed that Billy got his name right.

> AMOS
> Amos, that's right, Mr. Flynn. Amos.

[Billy questions Amos about why he filed for divorce, and he explains that he didn't believe Roxie's child was his.]

> BILLY
> Tell me something, Amos. Did you share a bed with your wife?

> AMOS
> Yes, sir. Every night.

Billy turns and points at Roxie.

> BILLY
> And you expect this jury to believe that you slept next to this woman every night without exercising your rights as a husband?

> AMOS (DEFENSIVE)
> Well, I could've if I wanted to.

> BILLY
> Oh, but you didn't.

> AMOS
> No, I did.

> BILLY
> Did what?

> AMOS
> Want to.

> BILLY
> But you didn't.

> AMOS
> Didn't what?

> BILLY
> What you wanted.

> AMOS
> Wait a minute. I'm gettin' confused here.

A showgirl winks at Roxie from the jury box. Billy looms over Amos, having lost his friendliness.

BILLY
Tell me, Hart. Did you ever question Roxie herself? Did you even bother to ask her if you were the father?

AMOS
No, sir...

Roxie turns back to the jury, with a wounded flutter.

BILLY
But you'd be willing to take her back, wouldn't you, if Roxie swore that you were the father of her child...which she does?

AMOS
She does?

Roxie nods, her eyes filled with tears.

BILLY
She does. No more questions. You can step down.

Amos leaves the witness box and moves over to Roxie.

AMOS
Oh, Rox...I'm so sorry.

They fall into each other's arms, as photographers immortalize the moment. Mary Sunshine dabs at her eyes with a handkerchief. Even some members of the jury are crying. Billy takes it all in with a proud smile.

INT. FANTASY COURTROOM - NIGHT
Billy stands on the judge's bench, wielding a circus whip. The showgirls have the run of the courtroom now, everyone twirling and spinning.

BILLY
GIVE 'EM THE OLD RAZZLE DAZZLE
RAZZLE DAZZLE 'EM

WOMEN
GIVE 'EM THE OLD RAZZLE
DAZZLE

Two showgirls drop rapidly on silks.

BILLY
SHOW 'EM THE FIRST RATE SORCERER YOU ARE

Billy teeters along a balustrade, using the Illinois state flag as a balancing pole. He makes his way back to the defense table.

BILLY (CONT'D)
LONG AS YOU KEEP 'EM WAY OFF BALANCE
HOW CAN THEY SPOT YOU GOT NO TALENTS?

Billy jumps onto the table and offers his hand to Roxie, who takes it. She stands on the table.

BILLY (CONT'D)
RAZZLE DAZZLE 'EM

Billy puts Roxie's hands in a ring.

WOMEN
RAZZLE DAZZLE 'EM

BILLY
RAZZLE DAZZLE 'EM

INT. COURTROOM - DAY (REALITY)
A long drum roll. Mary Sunshine whispers into a radio microphone.

MARY SUNSHINE
This is the moment we've been waiting for. Roxie Hart finally takes the stand in her own defense.

Roxie stands nervously.

INT. FANTASY COURTROOM - NIGHT
Roxie ascends on the ring and travels across the courtroom.

BILLY & WOMEN
AND THEY'LL MAKE YOU A STAR!

Fireworks shower down on the courtroom. Roxie gazes down, a little scared, as she is lowered into the witness box.

INT. COURTROOM - DAY
Roxie on the witness stand. The last finger snaps become the taps of the judge's gavel.

JUDGE
Order. Order. Proceed, Mr. Flynn.

BILLY
Roxie, I have here a statement in which you admit to having illicit relations with the deceased, Fred Casely. Is this statement true or false?

ROXIE
I'm afraid that's true.

BILLY

You're an honest girl, Roxie. When did you first meet Fred Casely?

ROXIE

When he sold Amos and me our furniture.

BILLY

And your personal relationship with him — could you tell the jury when that began?

ROXIE

When I permitted him to escort me home one night.

[Roxie delivers her rehearsed speech. She says that she fell into an adulterous relationship because she was unhappy. Amos worked long hours at the garage, but she wanted him at home with her. She admits to killing Casely, but insists that's she's no criminal.]

She collapses into tears. Billy hands her a handkerchief.

BILLY

There, there... Roxie, can you recall the night of January 14th?

ROXIE

Yes, sir. When Fred came over I told him my good news.

BILLY

What was that?

ROXIE

That Amos and me were gonna have a baby. And that it was all over between us.

BILLY

And what happened then?

ROXIE

Then? Oh, well, um...

She's forgotten her lines.

BILLY

Did he threaten you, Roxie?

HARRISON

Objection, Your Honor. Counsel is leading the witness.

JUDGE

Sustained.

BILLY

What did Casely say when you told him the news?

[Roxie claims that he said he'd kill her if she had Amos's baby.]

BILLY

Could you tell the audience...the jury...what happened next.

ROXIE

In his passion he tore off my robe and threw me on the bed. Mr. Hart's pistol was lying there between us.

BILLY

And then?

[Roxie says that they both reached for the gun and that she shot Casely to save Amos's unborn child.]

Roxie faints, sending the crowd to its feet. Billy rushes over to her.

ROXIE (CONT'D) (UNDER HER BREATH)
What a bullseye, huh?

In the back, Mary files her report directly from the courtroom, whispering into a radio microphone.

MARY SUNSHINE
There's pandemonium here in the courtroom....

INT. COOK COUNTY JAIL - MATRON'S OFFICE - DUSK
The matron and Velma are glued to the radio report. There's a bottle of bootleg whiskey and two shot glasses between them.

MARY SUNSHINE (V.O.)
Mrs. Hart's behavior throughout this ordeal has been truly extraordinary....

VELMA
I bet it has.

MARY SUNSHINE (V.O.)
Opening her eyes, she asks to borrow her attorney's handkerchief....

Velma's eyes narrow.

VELMA
Handkerchief?

MARY SUNSHINE (V.O.)
The poor child has had no relief. She looks around now, bewildered, seeming to want something. Oh, it's a glass of water.

VELMA
That's my bit! I told Billy I was gonna do that at my trial!

MARY SUNSHINE (V.O.)
She takes a tiny sip and it seems to revive her...but now her eyes flutter wildly...and she collapses like a crumpled rag doll. That's right, Mrs. Hart has fainted again. She slumps over, her chiffon dress up around her knees, revealing a glimpse of a blue garter with a rhinestone buckle.

VELMA
Mama, she stole my garter!

MARY SUNSHINE (V.O.)
I hear it was a wedding gift from her dear husband Amos.

Velma picks up the radio to throw it. The matron stops her.

MATRON
Velma, don't break my radio.

VELMA
First that slob steals my publicity, my lawyer, my trial date, and now my garter.

MATRON (NURSING HER OWN WOUNDS)
Well, whaddaya expect? These days, you get a little success, and it's good riddance to the people who put you there.

The matron snaps off the radio.

VELMA
There ain't no justice in the world. And there's nothing you can do about it.

MATRON
Aw, nerts to that. You think I got you up here just so you could listen to the radio?

She opens her desk drawer, takes out the familiar silver diary with Roxie's name on the cover.

MATRON (CONT'D)
You know, people write some interesting things when they think no one's lookin'.

Velma looks intrigued. We CUT TO:

INT. COURTROOM - DAY
Harrison stands, speaks in a thunderous voice.

HARRISON
The State calls a rebuttal witness.

Velma Kelly enters, dressed to the nines. Roxie and

Billy share a look of concern as Velma breezes past and takes the stand.

BAILIFF
You swear to tell the truth, the whole truth, and nothing but the truth, so help you God?

VELMA
And then some.

HARRISON
Would you state your name for the record?

VELMA
Velma Kelly.

HARRISON
Miss Kelly, will you please tell the court if the object I am holding is the one you happened to come upon in the defendant's jail cell.

He holds up the silver diary.

VELMA
Yes it is.

HARRISON
I submit this as Exhibit X. Roxie Hart's diary!

BILLY
I object! My client has never kept a diary, and even if she had, this would be invasion of privacy, violation of the Fourth Amendment, and illegal search without a warrant!

ROXIE
Yeah, and she broke the lock!

The court erupts in laughter. Billy's face reddens.

JUDGE
Well that settles that. I'll allow it. Proceed, Mr. Harrison.

Billy sits. Roxie leans across, whispers.

ROXIE
What's the big deal? It's just a lot of doodlings.

Harrison hands the diary to Velma.

HARRISON
If you would read for us, Miss Kelly.

VELMA
I haven't worked in a while.
(reads)
"What a laugh, pluggin' Fred Casely. The big baboon had it comin'. I'm just sorry I only got to kill him once."

The jury turns in horror to Roxie, who jumps out of her chair.

ROXIE
I never wrote that! You...she made it up!

Billy restrains her, as reporters and onlookers stand to get a better view. The judge pounds the bench with his gavel.

JUDGE
Order! Order! Mr. Flynn, please get control of your client.

BILLY
Sorry, Your Honor. It won't happen again.

ROXIE
But...

BILLY (UNDER HIS BREATH)
Sit down. You're only making it worse.

Billy eases Roxie into her chair. Harrison smiles smugly.

HARRISON
I have no more questions.

JUDGE
Your witness, Mr. Flynn.

Roxie turns to Billy, who takes a deep breath and stands. A hush falls over the courtroom.

INT. "STAGE" - NIGHT

The BANDLEADER leans into his microphone.

> **BANDLEADER**
> Ladies and gentlemen, a tap dance...

The spotlight finds Billy, who shields his eyes from the glare.

INT. COURTROOM - DAY

Billy stands opposite Velma, scanning the diary.

> **BILLY**
> Tell me, Miss Kelly. Did you make a deal with Mr. Harrison? Maybe get him to drop the charges against you in exchange for testifying here today?

> **VELMA**
> Well sure. I'm not a complete idiot.

The crowd laughs along with her. The COURT STENOGRAPHER taps on his keys, the rhythm leading into:

INT. "STAGE" - NIGHT

Billy eases into a simple step, which he repeats again and again. He's playing for time.

INT. COURTROOM - DAY

Billy is still skimming the pages.

> **BILLY**
> Good.

He nods, finally seeing something that sparks his interest.

> **BILLY** (CONT'D)
> Since you gave such an impressive perform-ance for Mr. Harrison, maybe you'd do me the same honor...

> **VELMA**
> I'd be delighted.

Billy hands the diary to Velma, points out a passage.

> **VELMA** (CONT'D) (READS)
> "Fred Casely assured me he'd get me an audition down at the Onyx. Then he reneged on his pledge and that was my motive for attacking him."

> **BILLY**
> Hmmm. That's a pretty fancy way of saying he was a big fat liar who welshed on a deal, so I shot him.

He takes the diary from Velma, reads.

> **BILLY** (CONT'D)
> "Amos accused me of having an affair, so I told him the charge was...erroneous."

HARRISON
Objection, Your Honor! Mr. Flynn is twisting this evidence to draw conclusions which are specious and...

BILLY
Erroneous?

HARRISON
Exactly!

Harrison catches himself but it's too late, he's fallen into the trap.

INT. "STAGE" - NIGHT
Billy loosens up, starting to get the hang of it.

INT. COURTROOM - DAY
Billy leans in close to Velma.

BILLY
Miss Kelly, do you know what the word 'perjury' means?

A flicker of anxiety in Velma's eyes.

VELMA
Of course.

BILLY
Do you also know that it's a crime? For example, if it turned out you knew this diary was a fake, well...

Velma tugs at her gloves.

BILLY (CONT'D)
...I'd hate to think of you rotting away in prison for another ten years, especially after you've just won your freedom.

VELMA
Look, all I know is what I was told.

The courtroom reacts to the revelation.

INT. "STAGE" - NIGHT
Billy's dance becomes more intricate. Trickier.

INT. COURTROOM - DAY
Billy turns to face the jury.

BILLY
So you didn't find this diary in Roxie's cell?

VELMA
No. Mama — Miss Morton gave it to me. She said someone sent it to her.

BILLY
Any idea who this mysterious benefactor might be?

VELMA
No. She didn't know.

BILLY
Alright, let's see if we can work this out. He's someone who writes about reneging on pledges and erroneous charges. Call me crazy, but doesn't that sound like a lawyer to you?

Roxie smiles, starting to understand what Billy is up to.

BILLY (CONT'D)
A lawyer who obviously had a sample of my client's handwriting. Mr. Harrison, didn't you ask Roxie to write out a confession for you?

HARRISON
Yes, but you're not suggesting that I'd tamper with evidence...

BILLY
Of course not. Don't be ridiculous. That's thoroughly and utterly absurd.
(a beat)
But now that you mention it...

The courtroom explodes.

INT. "STAGE" - NIGHT
Billy's dance explodes, a muscular display of determination and skill. The percussion gets louder.

INT. COURTROOM - DAY
Harrison jumps up, apoplectic.

HARRISON
Your Honor, this is outrageous....

BILLY
...outrageous, I know! To suggest that the prosecutor made a thieves' bargain with the notorious Velma Kelly...and then fabricated the very evidence that set her free...just so he could win another case and move one step closer to the Governor's mansion...why it's simply beyond all imagining, and that's why you'll never hear it coming from my lips!

INT. "STAGE" - NIGHT
Billy is whirling in circles across the stage now.

INT. COURTROOM - DAY

The judge bangs his gavel and Harrison sputters objections, but Billy rides right over them:

BILLY

No, it isn't even conceivable, but if it were — wouldn't it be time to say: Come clean, Mr. Harrison? Even in Chicago, this kind of corruption cannot stand! Will not stand!

JUDGE

Enough, Mr. Flynn!

BILLY

I agree, Your Honor, it is enough! The defense rests!

INT. "STAGE" - NIGHT

Billy finishes, smooth and silky. He takes a bow.

INT. RADIO SHOP - DOWNTOWN CHICAGO - DAY

PEDESTRIANS stand quietly in the doorway, straining to hear.

MARY SUNSHINE (V.O.)

Ladies and gentlemen, this is Mary Sunshine, reporting live from the Cook County courthouse. The city of Chicago has come to a complete standstill, as the "Trial of the Century" finally draws to a close.

INT. SPEAKEASY - DAY

A ball glides along a pool table, until a hand stops it. GANGSTER TYPES abandon a poker game and huddle around a radio at the end of the bar.

MARY SUNSHINE (V.O.)

Mrs. Hart sits quietly at the defense table, hands folded, wondering what fate has in store for her.

INT. WRIGLEY GUM FACTORY - MANAGER'S OFFICE - DAY

The MANAGER places a microphone next to the radio, allowing Mary's voice to be heard on the factory floor.

MARY SUNSHINE (V.O.)

And now a hush falls over the courtroom, as the twelve men of the jury file slowly back into the courtroom....

INT. COURTROOM - DAY

The courtroom is crammed, all eyes on the jury as they file into the box.

JUDGE

Gentlemen of the jury. Have you reached a verdict?

FOREMAN

We have, Your Honor.

MARY SUNSHINE

(quietly, into the microphone)
The jury has reached a verdict.

JUDGE
Will the defendant please rise?

Roxie and Billy stand.

JUDGE (CONT'D)
And what is your verdict?

EXT. COURTHOUSE - DAY
Newspapers are set in two piles at the corner newsstand. One headline announces: ACQUITTED! ROXIE HART IS INNOCENT! The other screams: CONVICTED! ROXIE HART IS GUILTY!

At a courthouse window, a CLERK waves a white handkerchief. The NEWSBOY picks up the first pile.

NEWSBOY
She's innocent! Roxie Hart is innocent!

Passersby grab for papers. The newsboy's shouts are suddenly drowned out by the SOUND of gunshots. On the courthouse steps, a WOMAN stands, revolver in hand, two DEAD BODIES at her feet.

NEWSBOY (CONT'D)
Roxie Hart is free! She's free!

The crowd abandons him, racing toward the scene of the crime.

INT. COURTHOUSE - HALLWAY - DAY
We MOVE through the human stampede thundering out of the courtroom, until we reach...

INT. COURTROOM - DAY
...Roxie, who runs after the departing reporters and photographers. Behind her, the judge and jurors file out.

ROXIE
Don't you want to take my picture? I'm the famous Roxie Hart. What's goin' on around here? Billy, what the hell happened?

BILLY
This is Chicago, kid. You can't beat fresh blood on the walls.

ROXIE
But what about my publicity? My name in the papers. I was countin' on that.

BILLY
You know, your gratitude is overwhelming. I just saved your life.

ROXIE
Yeah, you get five thousand dollars and I wind up with nothin'.

BILLY
Five? Actually it's ten, once I collect from Velma.

Ladies and gentlemen,
Miss Roxie Hart
says goodnight...

Roxie looks up in confusion. Billy takes her diary from the bailiff's desk.

BILLY (CONT'D)
Here's your blessed diary. Hope you don't mind, I added a few erroneous phrases. Sorry I couldn't tell you. Couldn't take a chance.

Roxie turns, checking to see if any reporters have come back.

BILLY (CONT'D)
Never lost a case.

Billy winks, takes his hat and starts out.

BILLY (CONT'D)
You're a free woman, Roxie Hart. And God save Illinois!

Billy leaves and Roxie is alone. Sorry, almost forgot. There's still Amos.

AMOS
Roxie?

ROXIE
What do you want?

AMOS
I want you to come home. You said you still wanted to. And the baby...

ROXIE
Baby? What baby? Jesus, what do you take me for? There ain't no baby!

AMOS
There ain't no baby?

ROXIE (SADLY, TO HERSELF)
They didn't even want my picture. I can't understand that. They didn't even want my picture.

Amos leaves. Roxie stares out the window. Through the window's wire mesh, we see the red lights of ambulances and police cars.

ROXIE (V.O.) (CONT'D)
IT'S GOOD, ISN'T IT?
GRAND, ISN'T IT?
GREAT, ISN'T IT?
SWELL, ISN'T IT?
FUN, ISN'T IT?
NOWADAYS

INT. "STAGE" - NIGHT
The bandleader steps into a spotlight.

BANDLEADER
Ladies and gentlemen, Miss Roxie Hart says goodnight....

Lights fade up, revealing Roxie standing far upstage, glamorous in a shimmering black gown.

ROXIE
THERE'S MEN, EVERYWHERE
JAZZ, EVERYWHERE
BOOZE, EVERYWHERE
LIFE, EVERYWHERE
JOY, EVERYWHERE
NOWADAYS
YOU CAN LIKE THE LIFE YOU'RE LIVING
YOU CAN LIKE THE LIFE YOU LIKE
YOU CAN EVEN MARRY HARRY
BUT MESS AROUND WITH IKE

As Roxie reaches the front of the stage, lights fade, leaving her standing in a single spot.

ROXIE (CONT'D)
AND THAT'S GOOD, ISN'T IT?
GRAND, ISN'T IT?
GREAT, ISN'T IT?
SWELL, ISN'T IT? FUN, ISN'T IT?
BUT NOTHING STAYS

The music soars as the spot closes in. There's a look of panic in Roxie's eyes as the stage goes black.

INT. THE ONYX - DAY
Roxie is auditioning now, accompanied by the bandleader, who plays the piano in his shirtsleeves. We have shifted from Roxie's fantasy to the reality of the actual club.

ROXIE
YOU CAN LIKE THE LIFE YOU'RE LIVING
YOU CAN LIVE THE LIFE YOU LIKE
YOU CAN EVEN MARRY HARRY
BUT MESS AROUND WITH IKE

CLUB OWNER (SPEAKING OVER THE SONG)
Didn't she kill a guy a while back?

STAGE MANAGER
Who can keep 'em straight anymore?

Behind them, a SHADOWY FIGURE watches from an alcove.

ROXIE (TRYING TO STAY FOCUSED)
AND THAT'S GOOD, ISN'T IT?

GRAND, ISN'T IT?
GREAT, ISN'T IT?

CLUB OWNER
(cuts her off)
That's great. We'll be in touch.

ROXIE
But I'm not quite finished yet —

He leaves, followed by the stage manager. The bandleader hands Roxie her sheet music, with an apologetic shrug.

BANDLEADER
Here's your music, hon.

ROXIE
Thanks.

He also leaves. As Roxie pulls on her coat:

WOMAN'S VOICE (O.S.)
You know, you're really pretty good.

Velma steps out of the shadows. Roxie turns away, gathers her things.

ROXIE
Right, that and a dime. What are you doing here?

VELMA
I heard you been makin' the rounds.

ROXIE
Yeah, well if it was up to you I'd be swingin' by now.

VELMA
C'mon, I always knew Billy'd get you off.

ROXIE (UNDER HER BREATH)
Oh yeah.

VELMA
You should learn how to put things behind you.

ROXIE
Oh thank you, I'll put that at the top of my list. Right after finding a job and an apartment with a john.

VELMA
Would you just shut up and listen to me?

Roxie leaves.

INT. ONYX - LOBBY - DAY
Roxie emerges through curtains into the lobby. Velma follows.

ROXIE
You know, you really are something, comin' here like some goddamn Queen Bee full of advice for a poor slob like me.
(turns)
Well get this straight, Miss Velma Kelly. I got

Chicago Theater

In the film's finale, Velma and Roxie join forces ("one jazz killer's nothin' these days, but two…") and hit the big time on stage at the Chicago Theatre. That required a bit of the ole razzle dazzle from the filmmakers, who had to turn back the clock on the 3,600-seat landmark theater, which opened in 1921.

A second unit crew spent a day in Chicago filming the downtown theater. But while the physical structure remained the same, the theater's surroundings had changed. A subway stop and adjacent El tracks and modern buildings needed to be removed, and the plastic marquee had to be replaced by a historically accurate steel marquee.

Back in Toronto, matte painters at special effects house Toybox eliminated the adjacent modern buildings, which were replaced with period architecture. A second unit in Toronto shot period extras and cars on a cobblestone street in front of a 200-foot green screen, using the same camera angle as the Chicago shoot.

Compositors at Toybox then combined the real theater with the extras and matte painting. Eight animators and six compositors worked for a total of six months at Toybox to create the Chicago Theatre and the street where Roxie lives. As Billy Flynn would say, "Give 'em the old hocus pocus."

LEFT: *Archival image of the Chicago Theater, 1927.*
ABOVE: *Special Effects plate (top) of the Chicago Theater, 2001 is transformed into the Chicago Theater, 1929 (bottom).*

179

a new life now, and the best thing about it is that it don't include you.

VELMA
Fine. I just thought we could help each other out.

ROXIE
Well you thought wrong, didn't you?

VELMA
Just listen to me, Roxie....

Velma grabs Roxie's arm, causing her to drop the sheet music. Velma crouches to pick it up, revealing a tear in her stockings.

VELMA (CONT'D)
I talked to this guy downtown. He says one jazz killer's nothin' these days, but two...

Velma stops when she sees that Roxie has noticed the stockings.

VELMA (CONT'D)
We could make a coupla hundred a week.

She hands Roxie the sheet music.

VELMA (CONT'D)
Think about it, Roxie. Our faces back in the papers. Our names on the marquee. Velma Kelly and Roxie Hart.

ROXIE
Shouldn't it be alphabetical?

VELMA
That could work.

Velma smiles, Roxie is in.

ROXIE
And come on, a coupla hundred? Don't you think we should be askin' for a thou?

VELMA
We're worth it.

ROXIE
It'll never work.

VELMA
Why not?

ROXIE
Because we hate each other.

VELMA
There's only one business in the world where that's no problem at all...

They both smile, twinkling with ambition and greed. The "All That Jazz" vamp starts.

BANDLEADER (V.O.)
Ladies and gentlemen, the Chicago Theater is proud to announce a first.

EXT. CHICAGO THEATER - NIGHT
A magnificently ornate vaudeville palace. We PULL BACK from letters formed by light bulbs, until they form a single word:

CHICAGO

INT. CHICAGO THEATER - NIGHT
A packed house in tuxes and jewels waits in nervous anticipation. The bandleader is onstage with his orchestra, all wearing white tuxes.

BANDLEADER
The first time anywhere there has been an act of this nature. Not only one little lady, but two! You've read about them in the papers and now here they are — Chicago's own killer dillers, those scintillating sinners — Roxie Hart and Velma Kelly.

Roxie and Velma rise into view, together at last. They wear matching white furs and identical wigs, Roxie's platinum, Velma's jet black.

ROXIE & VELMA
YOU CAN LIKE THE LIFE YOU'RE LIVING
YOU CAN LIVE THE LIFE YOU LIKE
YOU CAN EVEN MARRY HARRY
BUT MESS AROUND WITH IKE

“On some of the small set pieces that we built outside, we used a lot of exposed white bulbs. Chicago in the late '20s had a lot of signs that would be just a little black box with the name of the business, like 'Shoes,' written in white with the light bulbs embedded in it. And then we started playing with light bulbs in the Onyx Theater—it was something that Rob Marshall really loved. And with each musical number, we kept using more and more bulbs. For the final scene, we wondered how could we top all the light we'd used in the movie. So we came up with the idea of having a 20 foot by 30 foot wall of light bulbs—literally over 10,000 bulbs—and then having Roxie and Velma use their prop machine guns to shoot out the lights to spell their names.”

—JOHN MYHRE, PRODUCTION DESIGNER

The crowd is dotted with curiosity seekers who gape and titter at the infamous women. We also see Billy Flynn and Mama Morton, both wearing tuxes.

> **ROXIE & VELMA** (CONT'D)
> AND THAT'S GOOD, ISN'T IT?
> GRAND, ISN'T IT?
> GREAT, ISN'T IT?
> SWELL, ISN'T IT?
> FUN, ISN'T IT
> BUT NOTHING STAYS

Roxie and Velma twinkle and beam, a mutual admiration society. You'd never guess they can't stand each other.

> **ROXIE & VELMA** (CONT'D)
> IN FIFTY YEARS OR SO
> IT'S GONNA CHANGE, YOU KNOW
> BUT, OH, IT'S HEAVEN
> NOWADAYS

The MUSIC heats up as Roxie and Velma shed their furs and launch into the "Hot Honey Rag."

> **BANDLEADER** (O.S.)
> Okay, you babes of jazz. Let's pick up the pace. Let's make the parties longer, let's make the skirts shorter. Let's all go to hell in a fast car and keep it hot!

Roxie and Velma use prop machine guns as canes, then sign their names in bullet holes on the wall of lights behind them. The crowd cheers and throws flowers, as the women take their bows.

> **VELMA**
> Thank you. Me and Roxie would just like to thank you.

> **ROXIE**
> Thank you. Believe us, we could not have done it without you.

The audience seems to caress the two killers with its outstretched hands, almost smothering them with love.

> **ROXIE & VELMA**
> AND ALL THAT JAZZ!
> THAT JAZZ!

> The END

A MIRAMAX FILMS Presentation

CHICAGO

Directed by ....ROB MARSHALL
Screenplay by ....BILL CONDON
Produced by ....MARTIN RICHARDS
Executive Producers.............CRAIG ZADAN
NEIL MERON
Executive Producers..........SAM CROTHERS
BOB WEINSTEIN
Executive Producers...HARVEY WEINSTEIN
MERYL POSTER
JULIE GOLDSTEIN
JENNIFER BERMAN
Music by ....JOHN KANDER
Lyrics by ....FRED EBB
Director of Photography..DION BEEBE, ACS
Production Designer ....JOHN MYHRE
Editor....................................MARTIN WALSH
Costume Designer ....COLLEEN ATWOOD
Choreographed by ....ROB MARSHALL
Production Manager......JOYCE KOZY KING
First Assistant Director ...MYRON HOFFERT
Second Assistant Director GRANT LUCIBELLO
Co-Producer ....DON CARMODY
Choreographic Supervisor.....JOHN DELUCA
Associate Choreographers CYNTHIA ONRUBIA
JOEY PIZZI
Assistant Choreographer ....DENISE FAYE
Theatrical Lighting Design .....JULES FISHER
PEGGY EISENHAUER
Music Supervised and
Conducted by .... PAUL BOGAEV
Original Score Music by... DANNY ELFMAN
Additional Score Adaptation and Dance
Music Arrangements by... DAVID KRANE
Executive Music Producers.......... RIC WAKE
RANDY SPENDLOVE
Music Supervisor .... MAUREEN CROWE
Casting by.................. LAURA ROSENTHAL
& ALI FARRELL
Canadian Casting by.... TINA GERUSSI CDC

New York Dance Casting by
JAY BINDER CSA & JACK BOWDEN CSA

Dance Casting Canada by
STEPHANIE GORIN CDC, CSA

Based on the Musical Play "CHICAGO"

Directed and Choreographed for the Stage by
BOB FOSSE

Book of the Musical Play by
BOB FOSSE and FRED EBB

Produced on the Stage by
ROBERT FRYER, JAMES CRESSON
MARTIN RICHARDS

In Association with
JOSEPH HARRIS, IRA BERNSTEIN

Lyrics and Music Published by
UNICHAPPELL MUSIC INC.

Based on the Play by
MAURINE DALLAS WATKINS

CAST

Roxie Hart...................RENÉE ZELLWEGER
Velma Kelly.........CATHERINE ZETA-JONES
Billy Flynn.........................RICHARD GERE
Matron Mama Morton.......QUEEN LATIFAH
Amos Hart......................JOHN C. REILLY
Kitty Baxter ....LUCY LIU
Bandleader ....TAYE DIGGS
Harrison..............................COLM FEORE
Mary Sunshine.........CHRISTINE BARANSKI
Fred Casely ....DOMINIC WEST
Mona ....MYA HARRISON
June ....DEIDRE GOODWIN
Annie ....DENISE FAYE
Hunyak... EKATERINA CHTCHELKANOVA
Liz .... SUSAN MISNER
Stage Manager .... CLIFF SAUNDERS
Mrs. Borusewicz........... JAYNE EASTWOOD
Police Photographer........... BRUCE BEATON
Sergeant Fogarty .... ROMAN PODHORA
Newspaper Photographer .... ROB SMITH
Reporter.................... SEAN WAYNE DOYLE
Prison Clerk .... STEVE BEHAL
Prison Guard.......................... ROBBIE ROX
Nickie .... CHITA RIVERA
Bernie .... JOEY PIZZI
Ezekial Young........................ SCOTT WISE
Wilbur .... KEN ARD
Hunyak's Husband........... MARC CALAMIA
Veronica.................................... NIKI WRAY
Charlie........................ GREG MITCHELL
Al Lipschitz .... SEBASTIAN LaCAUSE
Billy's Assistant .... BRENDAN WALL
"Gun" Reporter #1 .... CLEVE ASBURY
"Gun" Reporter #2 .... RICK NEGRON
"Gun" Reporter #3............. SHAUN AMYOT
Billy's Secretary .... EVE CRAWFORD
Newsreel Announcer .... BILL CORSAIR
Auctioneer .... BILL BRITT
Sailor...........................GERRY FIORINI
Perfume Lady...................ELIZABETH LAW
Harry..............................JOSEPH SCOREN
Bare Woman #1.... MONIQUE GANDERTON
Bare Woman #2 .... APRIL MORGAN
Groin Reporter .... MARTIN MOREAU
Doctor .... CONRAD DUNN
Hospital Reporter .... CLEVE ASBURY
Bailiff .... JONATHAN WHITTAKER
Jury Foreman .... ROD CAMPBELL
Harrison's Assistant .... BRETT CARUSO
Judge...................... SEAN McCANN
Court Clerk.......................... JEFF CLARKE
Newsboy.................... PATRICK SALVAGNA
Woman Shooter .... KATHRYN ZENNA
Club Owner............................. JEFF PUSTIL
Female Dancers........... ROXANE BARLOW,
JOEY DOWLING, MELANIE GAGE,

MICHELLE JOHNSTON, CHARLEY KING,
MARY ANN LAMB, VICKY LAMBERT,
TARA NICOLE, CYNTHIA ONRUBIA,
KARINE PLANTADIT-BAGEOT,
JENNIFER SAVELLI, NATALIE WILLES,
KAREN ANDREW, KELSEY CHACE,
CATHERINE CHIARELLI,
THERESA COOMBE, LISA FERGUSON,
MELISSA FLERANGILE,
MICHELLE GALATI, SHERI GODFREY,
BRITTANY GRAY, KAREN HOLNESS,
AMBER-KELLY MACKERETH,
JODI-LYNN McFADDEN, FAYE RAUW,
RHONDA ROBERTS, LEIGH TORLAGE,
ROBYN WONG
Male Dancers... SHAUN AMYOT, KEN ARD,
CLEVE ASBURY, TED BANFALVI,
HARRISON BEAL, PAUL BECKER,
MARC CALAMIA, JEAN-LUKE COTÉ,
SCOTT FOWLER, EDGAR GODINEAUX,
BILLY HARTUNG, SEBASTIAN LaCAUSE,
DARREN LEE, TROY LIDDELL,
BLAKE McGRATH, GREG MITCHELL,
ROBERT MONTANO, RICK NEGRON,
SEAN PALMER, DESMOND RICHARDSON,
MARTIN SAMUEL, JASON SERMONIA,
JEFF SIEBERT, SERGIO TRUJILLO,
SCOTT WISE
Acrobats .... STACY CLARK BAISLEY,
MEGAN FEHLBERG, RACHEL JACOBS,
REBECCA LEONARD, ERIN MICHIE,
DANIELLE RUEDA-WATTS
Stunt Coordinator .... STEVE LUCESCU
Acrobat Coach..... DECKER LADOUCEUR –
CIRQUE SUBLIME
Rehearsal Unit Second Assistant Director
CATHERINE GOURDIER
Mr. Gere's Tap Steps Created by
CYNTHIA ONRUBIA
Producer Circle Co. Executives
DAN GALLAGHER, MICHAEL MILTON
Executive in Charge of Physical Production
JAKE MYERS
Executives in Charge of Post Production
JENNIFER LANE, LINDA BORGESON
Camera Operator......... PETER ROSENFELD
First Assistant Camera .... MARK CYRE
Second Assistant Camera ... NEIL TRAFFORD
Camera Loader .... MICHAEL CARR
Camera Trainees ... SERHAT H. YALCINKAYA
ZACHARY CASE
"B" Camera Operator .... ROGER FINLAY
"B" Camera First Assistant
YVONNE COLLINS
"B" Camera Second Assistant... BETH NOBES
"C" Camera Operator .... JOCK MARTIN
"C" Camera First Assistant... NOEL VERHOOG
"C" Camera Second Assistant... DENNIS KIM
Associate Editors .... SCOTT RICHTER
DAVID ROGOW
First Assistant Film/VFX Editor
ANDREW WEISBLUM
Apprentice Editor .... EDDIE NICHOLS

First Assistant Digital Editor (Toronto)
GARY FLUXGOLD
First Assistant Film Editor (Toronto)
RUSSELL LANGILLE
Second Assistant Film Editor (Toronto)
SONJA OBLJUBEK
Apprentice Editor (Toronto) CHRISTINE HARE
Post Production Supervisor ....JEFF ROBINSON
Post Production Coordinator.... ERICA HYATT
Art Director.................. ANDREW STEARN
Set Designers ..... GRANT VAN DER SLAGT
MICHAEL R. SHOCRYLAS
TOM CARNEGIE
First Assistant Art Directors
NANCEY PANKIW, WAYNE WIGHTMAN
Graphic Designer.......... PAUL GREENBERG
Illustrator .... SEAN BREAUGH
Art Department Coordinator.... BETH GILINSKY
Third Assistant Art Directors
BRAD MILBURN, ABBIE WEINBERG
Art Department Apprentice ... DOMINIKA PYK
Storyboard Artist .... RON HOBBS
Set Decorator............................ GORD SIM
Buyers.............................. MARLENE RAIN
BRENDA McCLENNIN
Lead Men...... KEITH SLY, DAN WLADYKA
On Set Dresser .... DAVID EVANS
Script Supervisor............. SUSANNA DAVID
Sound Mixer .... DAVID LEE
Boom Operator......... DENIS BELLINGHAM
Music Playback Operators ... DENIS TOUGAS
JASON McFARLING
BILL BRIDGES
Wardrobe Supervisor .... CORI BURCHELL
Key Costumer........ CHRISTINE CANTELLA
Wardrobe Buyer.............. IAN DRUMMOND
Set Supervisor.................. ANDRE SCHULZ
Assistant Set Supervisors.... WINDY KERWIN
DONNA BUTT
Head Cutter......................... DALE WIBBEN
Cutters .... LOREEN LIGHTFOOT
KAREN NASER
Principal Stitcher .... HAYDEE RAMIREZ
Seamstresses .... JANICE SKINNER,
RITTA KOLEVA, SUSAN MACLEOD
Dyeing/Breakdown....... TRELAWNIE MEAD
Wardrobe Production Assistant
HEATHER GOODCHILD
Ms. Zellweger's Dresser.... RENÉE BRAVENER
Ms. Zeta-Jones' Dresser....... GERRI GILLAN
Mr. Gere's Dresser .... TOMMY BOYER
Key Hair Stylist......... JUDI COOPER SEALY
Assistant Hair Stylists... VERONICA CIANDRE,
LUCY ORTON, PAULA FLEET
Key Make Up.................. JORDAN SAMUEL
Make Up Assistants ... PATRICIA KEIGHRAN
EDELGARD PFLUEGL
Hair Stylist for Ms. Zellweger
COLLEEN CALLAGHAN
Make Up for Ms. Zellweger
JORDAN SAMUEL
Hair Stylist for Ms. Zeta-Jones
KARYN L. HUSTON

Make Up for Ms. Zeta-Jones
CINDY WILLIAMS
Hair Stylist for Mr. Gere LYNDELL QUIYOU
Make Up for Mr. Gere.......... LUANN CLAPS
Technical Lighting Gaffer.... BERNIE BRANSTON
Technical Lighting Best Boy ... DAVE BREEZE
Virtuoso Programmer
MATTHEW KIRK HUDSON
Dimmer Board Operators... GEOFF FROOD,
DOUGLAS HOOK, DAVE REPPEN
Follow Spots .... DEAN MUTO,
WILLIAM MEADOWS, PAUL QUESNEL,
MARK LAPOINTE
Gaffer .... FRANCO TATA
Best Boy Electric .... DOUG BLACK
Electrics....................... ROBERT HANNAH,
GORD ELDRIDGE, ERIC HOLMES,
DON CAULFIELD, TONY ELDRIDGE
Genny Operator .... JOHN SZTEJNMILER
Rigging Gaffer...................... PAUL SPAVEN
Best Boy Electric .... BARRY GOODWIN
Rigging Electrics........... DAVE NICHOLSON
GRAEME RIVERS
Key Grip.................. MARK MANCHESTER
Best Boy Grip .... MALCOLM NEFSKY
Dolly Grip .... TRACY SHAW
Grips.... ROBERT VIGUS, RON RENZETTI,
JIM KOHNE, MONTY MONTGOMERIE
Key Rigging Grip .... ROBERT DAPRATO
Assistant Key Rigging Grip ... PETER DAPRATO
Rigging Grips .... GLEN GOODCHILD,
STEVE SHERIDAN, JEFF HEINTZMAN,
TONY DUBREUIL, GUY GERVAIS
Key Flyman .... ROB NARDI
Flyman .... ANDRE OUIMET
Property Master.... CHRISTOPHER GEGGIE
Assistant Property Master .... HENRY JESIAK
Property Buyer............... MICHAEL MEADE
Props Assistant .... BRIAN PATRICK
Special Effects Coordinator .... TED ROSS
Assistant Head Special Effects
DAVID REAUME
Special Effects Head On Set ... MARCUS RAIT
Special Effects Assistant Head On Set
BRAD LARKIN
Special Effects Pre-Rig Head
GORDON HUDSON
Assistant Head Pre-Rig Special Effects
SKYLAR WILSON
Special Effects Technicians .. TERRY DOYLE,
WAYNE PRIEST, STANI VESELINOVIC
Video Dubbing................ TONY MORRONE
Production Coordinator ... SHELLEY BOYLEN
Assistant Coordinator........ ANDREAS HASS
Travel Coordinator .... DANA L. RAMSAY
Production Secretary ..... MELISSA GIROTTI
Production Assistants .... ROBIN HAYMAN
SCOTT WOUDA
Third Assistant Director..... TYLER DELBEN
Training Assistant Directors
MICHAEL MANZATO
JOSEPH FINKLEMAN
MICHAELA HUDSON

Assistant to Mr. Marshall... ARTHUR ROSES
Trailer Assistant Directors ... ADAM BOCKNEK
BEVERLY MORGAN
Ms. Zeta-Jones' Dialect Coach... JOY ELLISON
Vocal Coach .... ELAINE OVERHOLT
Assistants to Mr. Richards
MARYANNE DITTMANN
MONIQUE BELL
Assistant to Mr. Meron & Mr. Zadan
MARK NICHOLSON
Assistant to Mr. Carmody ... SARAH MILLIKEN
Assistants to Mr. Harvey Weinstein
BEN FAMIGLIETTI, DAVID GREENBAUM,
ERIC ROBINSON
Assistant to Ms. Poster KELLY CARMICHAEL
Assistant to Ms. Zellweger
MEREDITH CHISLETT
Assistant to Ms. Zeta-Jones JENNIFER CÔTÉ
Assistant to Ms. Latifah ... LAWANDA BLACK
Ms. Zellweger's Stand In BROOK PATTERSON
Ms. Zeta-Jones' Stand In .... PATRIZ QUAS
Mr. Gere's Stand In .... GARY DOUGLAS
Supervising Sound Editor
MAURICE SCHELL, M.P.S.E.
Supervising Music Editor
ANNETTE KUDRAK
Re-Recording Mixers.... MICHAEL MINKLER
DOMINICK TAVELLA
Sound Effects Editors......... EYTAN MIRSKY
RICHARD P. CIRINCIONE
Assistant Sound Editor.............. JAY KESSEL
Dialogue Editor .... LAURA CIVIELLO
Supervising ADR Editor... GINA R. ALFANO
ADR Editors .... HAL LEVINSOHN, M.P.S.E.
LOUIS BERTINI, M.P.S.E.
Assistant ADR Editor.............. LYNN SABLE
Supervising Foley Editor .... JEFFREY STERN
Foley Editor .... BRUCE KITZMEYER
ADR Mixers .... DAVID BOULTON,
BOBBY JOHANSON, PAUL ZYDEL
ADR Recordists .... ALEX RASPA
KRISSOPHER CHEVANNES
BRIAN GALLAGHER
Foley Artist..................... NANCY CABRERA
Foley Recordists...................... PAUL ZYDEL
RYAN COLLISON
ALEXANDRA BALTARZUK
Machine Room Operators.... MIKE PATRICK
ROBERT OLARI
Music Editor.................. E. GEDNEY WEBB
Assistant Music Editors .... JAMIE LOWRY
GISBURG SMIALEK
Lip Sync Editors .... KENTON JAKUB
MISSY COHEN
Post Production Interns .. MATTHEW PRAET,
LISA LOTTI, MICHAEL ILASI,
SANDRA SILVERSTEIN,
DAVE ROSENBERG
Construction Coordinator....... PHIL TELLEZ
Head Carpenter/Foreman
JIM O'DONOGHUE
Assistant Head Carpenter........... MING YEE
Office Assistant .... SARAH ASHTON

Location Head Carpenters.... PAT McCAFFERY
TONY PARKIN
Key Metal Fabricator........ ALEX TELLNOW
First Assistant Metal Fabricator.
BOB NEWMAN
Metal Fabricators.......... KEVIN FORSTNER,
IVAN ALAMINA, AARON DINSMORE
Location Manager........... MARTY DEJCZAK
Assistant Location Manager.... DAVID McILROY
Location Production Assistants
MICHAEL HARLAND, BRETT MILLER
Carpenters/Laborers...............DAN BROWN,
RICARDO BURKHARDT,
GORD CASSELMAN, VINCE DONATO,
PAUL DZATKO, CHRIS HANSON,
PETE HARWOOD, SAL LARIZZA,
MIKE LOTOSKY, BRIAN LUMLEY,
BRIAN MURRAY, MIKE NEWTON,
TOM OSMOND, PAUL RAPATI, MYLES
ROTH, TOM SHEEHAN, BLAINE TWYNE
Key Scenic Artist............ JOHN BANNISTER
Assistant Scenic Artist....... JANET CORMAK
Head Painter....................... TIM CAMPBELL
Assistant Head Painter.......... LUKE GIBSON
Head Plasterer........... MICHAEL SHERWIN
Plasterers............................. RICK BROOKS
DOUG RENNIE
On Set Stand by Carpenter... CHUCK LORIOT
On Set Stand by Painter ..... BRAD FRANCIS
Painters .... ROB BROOKE, PAT CHARD,
JOHN FLYNN, GLENN LOCKE, DAVE
MYLES, VICTOR QUON, WERNER
SCHLATTER, KARL SCHNEIDER,
CHARLES SHARUN, MARK STAFFORD,
DAVID WATTS
Accountant .... DOROTHY PRECIOUS
First Assistant Accountant ... CAROL ROTHEL
Second Assistant Accountants
DARREN WILSON, ALOMA TAYLOR
Third Assistant Accountants
EVA MARIE MacGREGOR
REBECCA DAWES
Payroll Accountant ..... SANDY GALLOWAY
Payroll Assistant .... MICHELLE MONTGOMERY
Post Production Accountant ... JANE TSIGHIS
Video Assistants .... DANIELLE LEBLANC
BRENDAN BRESNAHAN
Stills Photographers... DAVID JAMES, RAFY
Unit Publicist................... RACHEL ABERLY
Transportation Coordinator
NORM HENDERSON
Driver Captain .... JOHNNY OZOLINS
Drivers ....RUDY BACCUCHI, PAT
BEAUDROW, JEFF BELL, JOHN BROWN,
JOHN BRUNT, JOHN COCKS,
DAVE COTTON, FRANK ELDRIDGE,
KEN FRENETTE, MATT GARLAND,
RON HINES, STUART HUGHES,
MICHAEL K. JONES,
SCOTT MAGEE, SHAUN MAGEE,
DON MORLEY, JEFF PEEBLES,
DOUG PERRY, BILL TATARYN,
MAURICE TREMBLAY

REHEARSAL UNIT
D.G.C. Trainees .... DAVID C. SPARKES
BARBARA McCULLAM

SECOND UNIT
Director .... JOHN DELUCA
First Assistant Director .... TOM QUINN
Second Assistant Director ... MICHELE RAKICH
Third Assistant Director .... JOEL HAY
D.G.C. Trainee ...:.. EDNEY HENDRICKSON
Director of Photography
PETER BENISON, C.S.C.
First Assistant Camera .... CAROLYN COX
Second Assistant.............. KIRSTA TEAGUE
Video Assist .... RICHARD PENGELLY
Key Grip .... TIM SAUDER
Best Boy Grip ... PETER SCHALAKOWSKYJ
Dolly Grip .... OWEN SMITH
Gaffer .... MICHAEL McDONALD
Best Boy Electric .... BOB HICKS
Make Up Artist........................... BRIAN HUI
Key Hair .... PAULA FLEET
Property Master .... MARK HARMAN
Assistant Props .... ANNA BOGGILD-SMITH
Script Supervisor........ JOANNE HARWOOD
Driver Captain....................... DON MORLEY
Main Truck Package Driver ... STEVE COUTO
Wardrobe Supervisor .... MONICA WIER

CHICAGO UNIT
Location Manager/Coordinator
BRADY BREEN
Director of Photography
MICHAEL KOHNHORST
Camera Technician...... ROBERT W. FAISON
Second Assistant Camera .... K.C. CAPEK
Key Grip............................. KELLY BORISY
Dolly Grip..................... JASON STORANDT

ADDITIONAL PHOTOGRAPHY
Line Producer .... JOHN ECKERT
Production Supervisor .... PASIA SCHONBERG
Production Coordinator .... BOB WIGGINS
Production Secretary............... AMY BARRIE
First Assistant Accountant
VERONICA MILLER
Art Director .... GRANT VAN DER SLAGT
Set Designer .... DAVID FREMLIN
Director of Photography
JAMES CHRESSANTHIS, A.S.C.
Theatrical Lighting by .... PAUL GALLO
Theatrical Lighting Assistant
PHILIP ROSENBERG
Gaffer .... RICHARD ALLEN
Key Grip................. MICHAEL O'CONNOR
Best Boy .... STEVE VAN DENZEN
Hair Stylist for Ms. Zellweger
DALE BROWNELL
Set Decorator.................. PAUL ROBINSON
Sound Mixer..................... ERV COPESTAKE
Transport Coordinator .... MAC DAY
Driver Captain........................... BOB SILLS

ADDITIONAL PHOTOGRAPHY
SECOND UNIT
First Assistant Director .... FELIX GRAY
Director of Photography........ JENS STURUP
Gaffer................................... RODDY KSUB
Best Boy Gaffer.................... MATT TAYLOR
Grip .... JOHN VRAKKING
Best Boy Grip .... ED LIPSCOMBE
Props Master..................... ROBERT CROSS
Transportation Captain...... KEVIN MURPHY
Hair Stylist .... VERONICA CIANDRE
Make Up .... KATHLEEN GRAHAM
Craft Service .... ANGELA PENNY
New York Casting Assistant
KRISTA BOGETICH
Extra's Casting..................... JANE ROGERS
Extra's Casting Assistants
DYLAINE BOVAIRD
ALLISON MACGILLIVRAY
Craft Service
STARCRAFT – DAVID KINNERSLY
Servers................. KEVIN PATRICK ALLEN,
SARI MIETTINEN, CORALIE NOTT,
JEREMY LADNER
Catering .... CAPERS CATERING,
SHAIRE STEVENSON, BY DAVID'S,
DAVID MINTZ, JOHN DOYLE
Production Legal
KAREN G. FAIRBANK, ESQ.
Production Legal Assistant BEBE REYNOLDS
Medical Therapists............ KEVIN DUGUAY,
KARLA McCONNELL, TERRI REYNOLDS,
PHIL LAMONT
Visual Effects Supervisor
RAYMOND GIERINGER
VP Visual Effects .... MICHAEL ELLIS
Visual Effects Executive Producer
ANDY SYKES
Visual Effects Producer   WENDY LANNING
Visual Effects Coordinator...... CASSIA BUSS
Data Wrangler .... KEVIN CHANDOO
On Set Supervision
RAYMOND GIERINGER, JASON SNEA
Animation Supervisor.......... LON MOLNAR
3D Animation by................ MARK DAVIES,
PAUL GEORGE, GEOFF SCOTT,
ALEX STEPHAN
Digital Matte Painting by ...... BOJAN ZORIC
Lead Digital Compositor .... JASON SNEA
Digital Compositing by...... DUG CLAXTON,
JAY FIELD, MARK GOLDBERG,
MICHAEL HATTON
Additional Compositing by... ALEX BOOTHBY,
MARJORIE KNIGHT, BRIAN REID
Digital Film Technicians .... ERIC MYLES
ANDREW PASCOE
2K Spirit Data Transfers .... WALT BILJAN
KENN ELLIOT
Visual Effects Department Manager
BRUCE JONES
VP of Engineering .... BILL VARLEY
Visual Effects Systems Integrator
KLAUS STEDEN

Assistant Systems Integrator MARCUS BEINER
CGI Developer ... MISHKA GORODNITZKY
ADRIAN GRAHAM
Additional Services Provided by.... TOYBOX,
MOTION CONTROL,
MEDALLION/PFA FILM & VIDEO
Additional Visual Effects and End Title
Design by ....CUSTOM FILM EFFECTS
Visual Effects Supervisor ... MARK DORNFELD
Title Designer .... LORI MILLER
Visual Effects Producer
SUSAN SHIN GEORGE
Digital Lead Artist .... LAURIE POWERS
Digital Artists .... STEVE CALDWELL,
SHAINA HOLMES, AMANI WILLIAMS,
CHETAN DESHMUKH
Digital Editorial .... ADAM GASS
Digital I/O Manager ...... DAVID SMITHSON
Opening Title Design and Additional
Visual Effects by ....BIG FILM DESIGN
Designer/Visual Effects Supervisor
RANDALL BALSMEYER
Visual Effects Producer... KATHY KELEHAN
Digital Artists .... J. JOHN CORBETT
AMIT SETHI
Opticals and Digital Effects by
FILM EFFECTS INC.
Compositors .... JOHN FURNIOTIS,
ALISON MIDDAUGH, ROBERT YOSHIOKA,
KEVIN McBRIDE
Additional Visual Effects by
FILM EAST VISUAL EFFECTS
Digital Effects Producer....... WALTER HART
Digital Effects Supervisor .... JIM RIDER
Inferno Compositor KENNETH BRADBURD
Digital Artist............. JENNIFER COSSETTO
VFX Scanning by CYNE-BYTE IMAGING INC.
Senior Production Supervisor ..... ALAN BAK
Technical Supervisor .... JEFF BAKER
Scanning and Recording... DRAKE CONRAD,
FELIX HEEB, CHRIS ROSS,
MARK TURESKI
Project Co-Ordinator....... RICK HANNIGAN
Production Co-Ordinator DIANA MADUREIA

CAST RECORDINGS
Produced by................................ RIC WAKE
RANDY SPENDLOVE
Vocal Arranger.................... PAUL BOGAEV
Orchestrations............ DOUG BESTERMAN
"Razzle Dazzle" Orchestrator
MICHAEL STAROBIN
Drummer............................ PERRY CAVARI
Recording Engineers .... JOEL MOSS
DAN HETZEL
Pro Tools Engineers .... GUSTAVO CELIS
JIM ANNUNZIATO
Mixing Engineer.................... DAN HETZEL
Second Engineer............. JIM ANNUNZIATO
London Music Sessions Recorded at
AIR STUDIOS
Studio Manager .... ALISON BURTON
First Assistant .... JOHN BAILEY

Second Assistant .... CHRIS BARRET
Technicals .... RICHARD BARRIE
SIMON KNEE
London Musicians' Contractor
ISOBEL GRIFFITHS
London Copyist .... VIC FRASER
Wake Productions Coordinator
MARC RUSSELL
Wake Productions Business Affairs
PAM ROUSAKIS
Wake Productions Accountant
BARBARA BERGER
Associate Music Supervisor
MATTHEW SULLIVAN

MUSICIANS
Trumpet...................... DERRICK WATKINS
Trombone .... PETE BEACHILL
Tuba................................ OWEN SLADE
Violin Soloist .... CHRIS GARRICK
Piano .... DAVID HARTLEY
Double Bass .... PAUL MORGAN
Drums .... PERRY CAVARI
Banjo/Jazz Guitar .... MITCH DALTON
Percussion .... GARY KETTLE
Reed 1: Soprano and Alto Sax/Clarinet
JAMIE TALBOT
Reed 2: Soprano, Alto and
Tenor Sax/Clarinet...... STAN SALTZMAN
Reed 3: Tenor and Baritone
Sax/Clarinet/Bass Clarinet ALAN BARNES
RAY SWINFIELD
Toronto Vocals Recorded at
METALWORKS STUDIO
New York Additional Background Vocals
Recorded at.................AVATAR STUDIOS
Music Mixed at COVE CITY SOUND STUDIOS
Soundtrack Mastered by GREG CALBI AT
STERLING SOUND, NEW YORK CITY

Female Ensemble........ROXANNE BARLOW,
DANA CALITRI, KATE COFFMAN-LLOYD,
LAURA DEAN, MARGARET DORN,
JOCELYN DOWLING, MELANIE GAGE,
CAPATHIA JENKINS, CHARLEY KING,
MARY ANN LAMB, VICKY LAMBERT,
AUDREY MARTELLS, TARA NICOLE,
CYNTHIA ONRUBIA, SARA RAMIREZ,
NICKY RICHARDS

Male Ensemble ....SHAUN AMYOT,
CLEVE ASBURY, HARRISON BEAL,
DENNIS COLLINS, DARIUS DE HAAS,
WILLIE FALK, SCOTT FOWLER,
EDGAR GODINEAUX, BILLY HARTUNG,
CURTIS KING, DARREN LEE,
ROBERT MONTANO, RICK NEGRON,
SEAN PALMER, JOEY PIZZI,
DESMOND RICHARDSON,
TIMOTHY SHEW, JEFF SIEBERT,
FONZIE THORNTON, ERIC TROYER
Original Score Music Written & Produced by
DANNY ELFMAN

Music Editor for Danny Elfman
ELLEN SEGAL, M.P.S.E.
Assistant Original Score Music Editors
ANNE POPE, SHIE ROZOW
Original Score Music Published by
MIRAMAX FILMS MUSIC (BMI)
Original Score Music Conducted by
STEVE BARTEK
Orchestrations by .... STEVE BARTEK
BRUCE FOWLER
Original Score Music Recorded and Mixed by
DENNIS SANDS
Recordist .... GREG DENNEN
MIDI Supervision & Preparation by
MARC MANN
Tech Support by .... NOAH SNYDER
Music Preparation by .... JOANN KANE
Original Score Music Orchestra
Contracted by .... THE MUSIC TEAM
DEBBIE DATZ-PYLE
Original Score Music Recorded and Mixed at
WARNER BROS. EASTWOOD
SCORING STAGE
Technical Engineer........... RYAN ROBINSON
Scoring Stage Crew .... RICH WHEELER
BARRY FAWCETT
Additional Song/ Score Adaptations
Conducted by .... DOUG BESTERMAN
Additional Score Recorded at
PARAMOUNT PICTURES SCORING
STAGE M

"OVERTURE/AND ALL THAT JAZZ"
Music by John Kander
Lyrics by Fred Ebb
Performed by Catherine Zeta-Jones
Renée Zellweger, Taye Diggs
Published by Unichappell Music, Inc. (BMI)

"WHEN YOU'RE GOOD TO MAMA"
Music by John Kander
Lyrics by Fred Ebb
Performed by Queen Latifah
Published by Unichappell Music, Inc. (BMI)

"CELL BLOCK TANGO"
Music by John Kander
Lyrics by Fred Ebb
Performed by Catherine Zeta-Jones
Susan Misner, Denise Faye, Deidre Goodwin,
Ekaterina Chtchelkanova, Mya Harrison
Published by Unichappell Music, Inc. (BMI)

"CHICAGO"
Written by Fred Fisher
Published by Sony Music
and EMI Music Publishing, ASCAP

"ROXIE"
Music by John Kander
Lyrics by Fred Ebb
Performed by Renée Zellweger
Published by Unichappell Music, Inc. (BMI)

"ME AND MY BABY"
Music by John Kander
Lyrics by Fred Ebb
Published by Unichappell Music, Inc. (BMI)

"RAZZLE DAZZLE"
Music by John Kander
Lyrics by Fred Ebb
Performed by Richard Gere
Published by Unichappell Music, Inc. (BMI)

"NOWADAYS/HOT HONEY RAG"
Music by John Kander
Lyrics by Fred Ebb
Performed by Renée Zellweger,
Catherine Zeta-Jones
Published by Unichappell Music, Inc. (BMI)

"RAISIN' THE ROOF"
Written by Dorothy Fields
and Jimmy McHugh
Published by Aldi Music Company
and EMI Music Publishing, ASCAP

"FUNNY HONEY"
Music by John Kander
Lyrics by Fred Ebb
Performed by Renée Zellweger,
John C. Reilly
Published by Unichappell Music, Inc. (BMI)

"ALL I CARE ABOUT IS LOVE"
Music by John Kander
Lyrics by Fred Ebb
Performed by Richard Gere
Published by Unichappell Music, Inc. (BMI)

"WE BOTH REACHED FOR THE GUN"
Music by John Kander
Lyrics by Fred Ebb
Performed by Richard Gere,
Renée Zellweger, Christine Baranski,
Cleve Asbury, Rick Negron, Shaun Amyot
Published by Unichappell Music, Inc. (BMI)

"I CAN'T DO IT ALONE"
Music by John Kander
Lyrics by Fred Ebb
Performed by Catherine Zeta-Jones
Published by Unichappell Music, Inc. (BMI)

"MR. CELLOPHANE"
Music by John Kander
Lyrics by Fred Ebb
Performed by John C. Reilly
Published by Unichappell Music, Inc. (BMI)

"TAP DANCE"
Written and Performed by Perry Cavari

"NOWADAYS"
Music by John Kander
Lyrics by Fred Ebb

Performed by Renée Zellweger
Published by Unichappell Music, Inc. (BMI)

"I MOVE ON"
Music Coordinator TAMAR CHAMMOU

"EXIT MUSIC"
Music by John Kander
Published by Unichappell Music, Inc. (BMI)

Soundtrack Available on Epic/SONY
SOUNDTRAX

Richard Gere's singing and dancing
performed by RICHARD GERE

Renée Zellweger's singing and dancing
performed by RENÉE ZELLWEGER

Catherine Zeta-Jones' singing and dancing
performed by CATHERINE ZETA-JONES

Background Voices......... DAVID KRAMER'S
LOOPING GROUP
Banking Services .... HSBC BANK, USA
Color Timer .... CHRIS HINTON
Color by .... DELUXE TORONTO
Dolby Sound Consultant THOMAS KODROS
Insurance .... RICHARD EISENBERG
ERIC SHONZ & KERI WINTERS
AON/RUBEN WINKLER
ENTERTAINMENT INSURANCE BROKERS
Lab Services
DELUXE LABORATORIES, TORONTO
Mixed at .... SOUND ONE, INC.
Negative Cutter .... CATHERINE RANKIN
Payroll Service
ENTERTAINMENT PARTNERS, INC.
Post Production Accounting Services
R.C. BARAL
Video Dailies .... ENTERTAINMENT POST
Voice Casting .... DAVID KRAMER
Camera Lighting and Grip Equipment
WILLIAM F. WHITE LIMITED
ARRI CAM

"AND ALL THAT JAZZ/END CREDITS"
Music by John Kander
Lyrics by Fred Ebb
Performed by Catherine Zeta-Jones
Published by Unichappell Music, Inc. (BMI)
Music by John Kander
Lyrics by Fred Ebb
Performed by Catherine Zeta-Jones,
Renée Zellweger
Published by Unichappell Music, Inc. (BMI)

Footwear
CAPEZIO SHOES/BALLET MAKERS INC.
LADUCCA SHOES, NYC
Furs for Ms. Zellweger & Ms. Zeta-Jones
Provided by .... DENNIS BASSO FURS
Automated Lighting Provided by VARI*LITE

Post Production Film Equipment
PIVOTAL POST
SOUND ONE
Selected Jewelry.... NEIL LANE ANTIQUE &
ESTATE JEWELERY
Stock Footage .... F.I.L.M. ARCHIVES
GETTY IMAGES
Newsreel Music Courtesy of ABCNews
VideoSource

Dedicated to
BOB FOSSE, GWEN VERDON
and ROBERT FRYER

Special Thanks ....RALPH BURNS
VICKI CHERKAS
THE CITY OF TORONTO
SAM COHN
JIM GARDNER
MICHAEL GENDLER
JOHN HADITY
PETER HOWARD
RACHEL HUDGINS
MICHAEL LUISI
ONTARIO MEDIA DEVELOPMENT
CORPORATION
MAURA POWELL
JAY RUBIN
ROBERT A. SEIDENBERG
GARY TILLMAN
WILLIAM F. WHITE AND THE ARRI CAM
NO. 39516

In Association With KALIS
Productions GmbH & Co. KG

Copyright © 2002 KALIS
Productions GmbH & Co. KG

All Rights Reserved.

This motion picture was created by KALIS
Productions GmbH & Co. KG for purposes
of copyright law in the United Kingdom.
While this motion picture is based upon a
true story, certain characters' names have
changed, some main characters have been
composited or invented and a number
of incidents fictionalized.

Director/choreography ROB MARSHALL served in the same capacities on the Disney/ABC musical *Annie*, starring Academy Award®-winning actress Kathy Bates, Tony Award-winning actors Alan Cummings, Audra McDonald, Kristin Chenoweth, and Victor Garber, as well as Alicia Morton, who played the title role. The telefilm garnered huge ratings (the top rated made-for-TV for 1999) and a host of accolades, including a Peabody Award, a *TV Guide* Award, 12 Emmy® nominations, including Best Director and Choreographer, and a DGA Award nomination for Best Director. Prior to that, Marshall directed and choreographed the Broadway production of *Little Me*, starring Martin Short. He made his directorial debut co-directing the critically hailed Kander and Ebb musical *Cabaret*, which earned nominations for an Outer Critics' Circle Award, a Tony Award and a Drama Desk Award. He went on to direct *Promises, Promises* for the City Center Encores series. He also directed the Long Beach Civic Light production of *Chicago*, winning a Drama-Logue Award. Other choreography credits include Tim Robbins' film *Cradle Will Rock*, the Emmy®-nominated movies of the week *Cinderella*, featuring Whoopi Goldberg and Whitney Houston, and *Mrs. Santa Claus*. His Broadway choreography credits include the revival of *A Funny Thing Happened on the Way to the Forum*, directed by Jerry Zaks and starring Nathan Lane and Whoopi Goldberg, which earned an Outer Critics' Circle Award nomination; Blake Edward's stage incarnation of *Victor/Victoria*, which gained a Drama Desk Award nomination; and *Company*, which was also nominated for an Outer Critics' Circle Award. He choreographed the Broadway revival of *Damn Yankees*, which received a Tony Award nomination and an Outer Critics' Circle Award. He also choreographed Hal Prince's Broadway production of *Kiss of the Spider Woman*, as well as the London and Vienna incarnations. Marshall is a graduate of Carnegie-Mellon University.

Screenwriter BILL CONDON wrote and directed *Gods and Monsters*, starring Ian McKellen, Brendan Fraser, and Lynn Redgrave, for which Condon earned the Academy Award® for Best Adapted Screenplay. The National Board of Review named *Gods and Monsters* the best film of 1998. Born in New York City, he attended Columbia University where he received a degree in philosophy. An article he wrote for *Millimeter* Magazine brought him to the attention of producer/director Michael Laughlin, for whom Condon wrote his first two features, *Strange Behavior* and *Strange Invaders*. Condon made his directing debut with *Sister, Sister*, starring Jennifer Jason Leigh, Judith Ivey, and Eric Stoltz. He went on to direct several independent features and cable movies, such as *White Lie*, starring Gregory Hines, and *Murder 101*, for which he won an Edgar Award from the Mystery Writers of America.

Executive producers CRAIG ZADAN and NEIL MERON head the company Storyline Entertainment and under its aegis, they have produced many acclaimed projects that have brought the company, among other accolades, two Peabody Awards, 53 Emmy® nominations, and nine Golden Globe nominations.

The duo recently produced *Life with Judy Garland: Me and My Shadows*, which was both a critical and ratings success. It received 13 Emmy® nominations, including Outstanding Miniseries. It also recently won an AFI Award and its star, Judy Davis, earned a Golden Globe nomination. Of the 256 films of the season, it was the highest rated movie or miniseries of the year. It also won the Television Critics Association Award for Best Movie, Miniseries or Special.

Zadan and Meron also produced the update of *Brian's Song*, which aired to great ratings and acclaim. Previously, they produced the biographical telefilm *The Three Stooges*, with producing partners Mel Gibson and Bruce Davey's Icon Television. *The Three Stooges* was the highest-rated original programming in that Monday time slot in over 4 years, reaching over 16.5 million viewers.

Storyline's production of *The Beach Boys: An American Family* earned three Emmy® nominations, including Best Miniseries. It was the highest rated miniseries of the season. The film's kudos included

a DGA Award, a CAS Award for Outstanding Sound Mixing and an Eddie Award for Best Editing.

Storyline collaborated with Rob Marshall to executive produce the new televised version of the musical *Annie*. It won the *TV Guide* Award for Favorite TV Movie or Miniseries, the Peabody Award and two Emmy® awards. Director Rob Marshall received an Emmy® nomination, as did one of its stars, Kathy Bates, who also earned a Golden Globe nomination and a SAG nomination and won the American Comedy Award for Best Actress. *Annie* garnered 12 Emmy® nominations in total, including Outstanding Made for Television Movie, and was nominated by the Television Critics Association for Best TV Movie, Miniseries. They also worked with Marshall on Rodger's and Hammerstein's *Cinderella*, which Marshall choreographed and Zadan and Meron executive produced. The critically acclaimed television musical, which starred Whitney Houston, Brandy, Whoopi Goldberg, Jason Alexander, and Bernadette Peters, received the highest ratings for ABC in over a decade, reaching over 60 million viewers. The production also garnered seven Emmy® nominations, including Outstanding Special of the Year.

Storyline also produced the television movie *Flowers for Algernon*, based on the novel by Daniel Keyes, starring Matthew Modine and Kelli Williams. They also produced *Forget Me Never*, for which Mia Farrow was nominated for a Golden Globe for Best Actress. The film also co-starred Martin Sheen.

What Makes a Family was a historic lesbian custody drama for Lifetime Television starring Brooke Shields, Cherry Jones, Anne Meara and Whoopi Goldberg. Barbra Streisand, Whoopi Goldberg, and Cis Corman were also executive producers. This film was nominated for the 2001 Humanitas Prize for Best Television Cable Movie.

Zadan and Meron also produced, with partners Barbra Streisand, Glenn Close, and Cis Corman, *Serving in Silence: The Margarethe Cammemeyer Story*. This landmark NBC movie starred Close and Judy Davis. The film received six Emmy® nominations and won three: Best Actress for Close, Best Supporting Actress for Davis, and Best Screenplay for Alison Cross. Additionally, the show was nominated for three Golden Globe Awards for Best Picture, Best Actress, and Best Supporting Actress, and won the coveted National Education Association Award for the Advancement of Learning Through Broadcasting. The producers also won the prestigious Peabody Award for Outstanding Achievement in Broadcasting and were the recipients of the Lambda Liberty Award as well as the GLAAD Media Award. The show was also nominated for awards from The Producers Guild of America, The Writers Guild of America and The Screen Actors Guild.

Their first television event was *Gypsy*, a three-hour CBS movie musical, starring Bette Midler. *Gypsy* was a ratings and critical triumph (reaching an audience of more than 36 million viewers) and was nominated for 12 Emmy® Awards including Outstanding Made-For-TV Movie (the first such nomination for a film musical in the Academy's history). The show was also nominated for three Golden Globe Awards including Best Telefilm. Midler won both the Golden Globe for Best Actress, and the National Board of Review Award for Best Performance of the Year on Television. The show was also nominated for the Producers Guild of America Award, the Directors Guild of America Award, and the ACE Award. Their film credits include the comedy *My Fellow Americans*, starring Jack Lemmon and James Garner.

Producer MARTIN RICHARDS heads the film and theatrical production company, The Producer Circle, which he founded with his wife Mary Lea Johnson in 1976. Together, they produced some of America's best-loved Broadway and off-Broadway plays, as well as several well-regarded and popular movies. One of his many theatrical works includes the original Broadway production of *Chicago*, which he co-produced. *Chicago* earned 11 Tony Awards and was named Best Musical in London and Los Angeles. He also co-produced the Obie Award-winning *Dylan*; *The Norman Conquests*, which received the Outer Critics Circle Award; *La Cage aux Folles*, which won six Tony

Awards, including Best Musical; and *The Will Rogers Follies*, which Tommy Tune directed and choreographed. *The Will Rogers Follies* also won six Tony Awards, including Best Musical. He co-produced *The Best of Friends*, with Michael Douglas; *Sally Marr...and her Escorts*, starring Joan Rivers who received a Tony nomination; and *The Life*, which won The Drama Desk, The Outer Critics Circle, and The Drama League Awards for Best Musical. His recent production of *The Sweet Smell of Success*, directed by Nicholas Hytner and starring John Lithgow, opened in Chicago and traveled to Broadway. Other theater productions include *On the Twentieth Century*, directed by Harold Prince, which won five Tony Awards; *Sweeney Todd*, also directed by Prince, which won eight Tony Awards, including Best Musical; Beth Henley's *Crimes of the Heart*; *Foxfire*, for which Jessica Tandy won the Best Actress Tony Award; *Grand Hotel*, directed and choreographed by Tommy Tune, which won five Tony Awards; and the off-Broadway musicals *March of the Falsettos* and *Mayor*. Richards' film productions include *The Boys from Brazil*, *The Shining*, and *Fort Apache, The Bronx*.

Production designer JOHN MYHRE designed the recent Michael Mann biopic *Ali*, starring Will Smith, and the science fiction hit *X-Men*. He earned an Academy Award® nomination for his work on *Elizabeth* as well as BAFTA, Golden Satellite Award and American Society of Motion Picture and Television Art Directors Award nominations. Other credits include *Anna Karenina*, *Lawn Dogs*, *Vanishing Point*, *Foxfire*, *Airborne*, and *Puppet Master*. As an art director, his credits include *Immortal Beloved*, *What's Eating Gilbert Grape?*, *Blind Fury*, and *Amazing Grace & Chuck*.

Costume designer COLLEEN ATWOOD received her third Academy Award® nomination for Tim Burton's *Sleepy Hollow*. She also collaborated with Burton on *Planet of the Apes*, *Mars Attacks!*, *Edward Scissorhands*, and *Ed Wood*. She also worked on *The Mexican*. For director Jonathan Demme, Atwood designed costumes for *Married to the Mob*, *The Silence of the Lambs*, *Philadelphia*, and *Beloved*, the latter earning her a second Academy Award® nomination. Atwood's credits also include Tom Hanks' directorial debut, *That Thing You Do!*, as well as *Gattaca*, *Wyatt Earp*, *Lorenzo's Oil*, *Rush*, *Torch Song Trilogy*, *Someone to Watch Over Me*, and *Manhunter*. Atwood received her first Oscar nomination for Gillian Armstrong's *Little Women*.

Cinematographer DION BEEBE recently photographed *Charlotte Gray*. He has twice been recognized by the Australian Cinematographers Society, winning the Award of Distinction for the feature film *Praise* and in 1997 the Golden Tripod for the short film *Down Rusty Down*. In 1995, he won the Australian Film Critics Circle Awards for Best Cinematography for *What I Have Written* and has twice been nominated by the Australian Film Institute for his cinematography on *Praise* and *What I Have Written*. He also shot Jane Campion's *Holy Smoke*, starring Kate Winslett and Harvey Keitel, and *Equilibrium*, directed by Kurt Wimmer, starring Christian Bale and Emily Watson.

Editor MARTIN WALSH's other films include *Thunderbirds* (Universal/Working Title Pictures), *Bridget Jones' Diary* (Miramax), *Whatever Happened To Harold Smith?* (W11 Films), *Mansfield Park* (Miramax), *Hilary and Jackie* (Miramax), *The Mighty* (Miramax), *Welcome to Woop Woop* (Samuel Goldwyn Co.), *For Roseanna* (Fine Line), *Feeling Minnesota* (Jersey Films), *Hackers* (United Artists), *Funny Bones* (Suntrust), *Backbeat* (Scala Prods.), *Bad Behaviour* (Parallax), *Wild West* (Initial/Channel 4), *Hear My Song* (Limelight Films), *The Krays* (Fugitive Films), *The Fifteen Streets* (Worldwide TV/TYNE Tees), *Courage Mountain* (Stonebridge), and *The Wolves of Willoughby Chase* (Zenith).

Chicago:
acknowledgments

ACKNOWLEDGMENT OF PERMISSIONS: We are grateful to the publishers and other copyright holders named below for permission to reprint artwork from these previously published works. Artwork appears on the pages listed.

Page 22: DN-0084621. Photograph by *Chicago Daily News*. Used by permission of the Chicago Historical Society. **23:** DN-085378. Photo by *Chicago Daily News*. Used by permission of the Chicago Historical Society. **24:** Used by permission of Billy Rose Theatre Collection; The New York Public Library for the Performing Arts; Astor, Lenox, and Tilden Foundations. **25:** Copyright 1924 by Chicago Tribune Company. All rights reserved. Used with permission. **26:** Copyright 1924. Chicago Tribune Company. All rights reserved. Used with permission. **27 (top):** ICHi00462. Photograph by Copelin. Used by permission of the Chicago Historical Society. **27 (bottom right):** DN-0083971. Photograph by *Chicago Daily News*. Used by permission of the Chicago Historical Society. **27 (bottom left):** DN-76,798. Photograph by *Chicago Daily News*. Used by permission of the Chicago Historical Society. **31 (top):** Photograph by Martha Swope. Used with permission. **31 (bottom):** Photograph by Martha Swope. Used with permission. **34 (top):** Work Projects Administration Poster Collection (Library of Congress). **34 (bottom):** Work Projects Administration Poster Collection (Library of Congress). **56-57:** © Francis G. Mayer/CORBIS. **57 (inset):** Copyright Museum of the City of New York. Byron Collection, 41.420.383. **66:** Copyright 1987 Flammarion, Paris. All reprint rights copyright Mme. G. Brassaï, 1987. **93:** Copyright 2003 Man Ray Trust/Artists Rights Society (ARS), NY/ADAGP, Paris/Telimage. **103:** DN-0080572. Photograph by *Chicago Daily News*. Used by permission of the Chicago Historical Society. **179:** ICHi-10987. Photograph by Kaufmann & Fabry. Used by permission of the Chicago Historical Society.

The publisher has made every effort to contact copyright holders; any errors or omissions are inadvertent and will be corrected upon notice in future reprintings.

The publisher Esther Margolis wishes to thank the following for their special contributions to the creation of this book:

At Miramax Films: Jennifer Berman, David Bloch, Christopher Brescia, Bradley Buchanan, Jonathan Burnham, Jason Cassidy, Devereux Chatillon, Pamela Cruz, Kenn Doza, Christine Edwards, Julie Goldstein, Heather Johnson, Holly Landon, Michael Luisi, Meryl Poster, Kristin Powers, Lori Sale, Maya Schindler, Lori Shamah, Robert Seidenberg, Kathryn Tucker, and Joe Verciglio. At ICM: Sam Cohn and Maarten Kooij. At Producer Circle Co.: Michael Milton and Sam Crothers. Also, Christopher Measom of Night & Day Design, and at Newmarket Press: Frank DeMaio, Keith Hollaman, Shannon Berning, Kelli Taylor, Chris Cousino, Harry Burton, and Heidi Sachner. And most of all, our writer Peter Kobel and designer Timothy Shaner, and, of course, the contributors Rob Marshall, Bill Condon, and Martin Richards.

SOUNDTRACK AVAILABLE ON EPIC/SONY MUSIC SOUNDTRAX   EPIC   SONY MUSIC SOUNDTRAX